ACKNOWLEDGMENTS

The author wishes to thank the following people for their help in supplying background material for this book:

Art Popham and Monte Moore, of the Oakland Athletics, Roger Ruhl, of the Cincinnati Reds, Bob Hope, of the Atlanta Braves, Marty Appel, of the New York Yankees, as well as the publicity departments of all four teams; Bucky Albers, of the Dayton *Journal-Herald*; the publicity department at Arizona State University; Kevin Fitzgerald at *Sport* Magazine; Chuck Mehelich and Bob Trimble, of Cheltenham High School; Brooks Moser, of Southeast High School; and Mr. and Mrs. Ted Bench, Mr. and Mrs. Robert Murcer, Dick Williams, Ralph Houk, Tom Greenwade, Bobby Winkles and Dave Gunter.

At Bat!
Aaron · Murcer
Bench · Jackson

Bill Gutman

tempo
books

GROSSET & DUNLAP
Publishers   New York

Copyright © 1973 by Bill Gutman
All Rights Reserved
ISBN: 0-448-5566-X

Tempo Books is registered in the U. S. Patent Office
Published simultaneously in Canada

Printed in the United States of America

For Beth

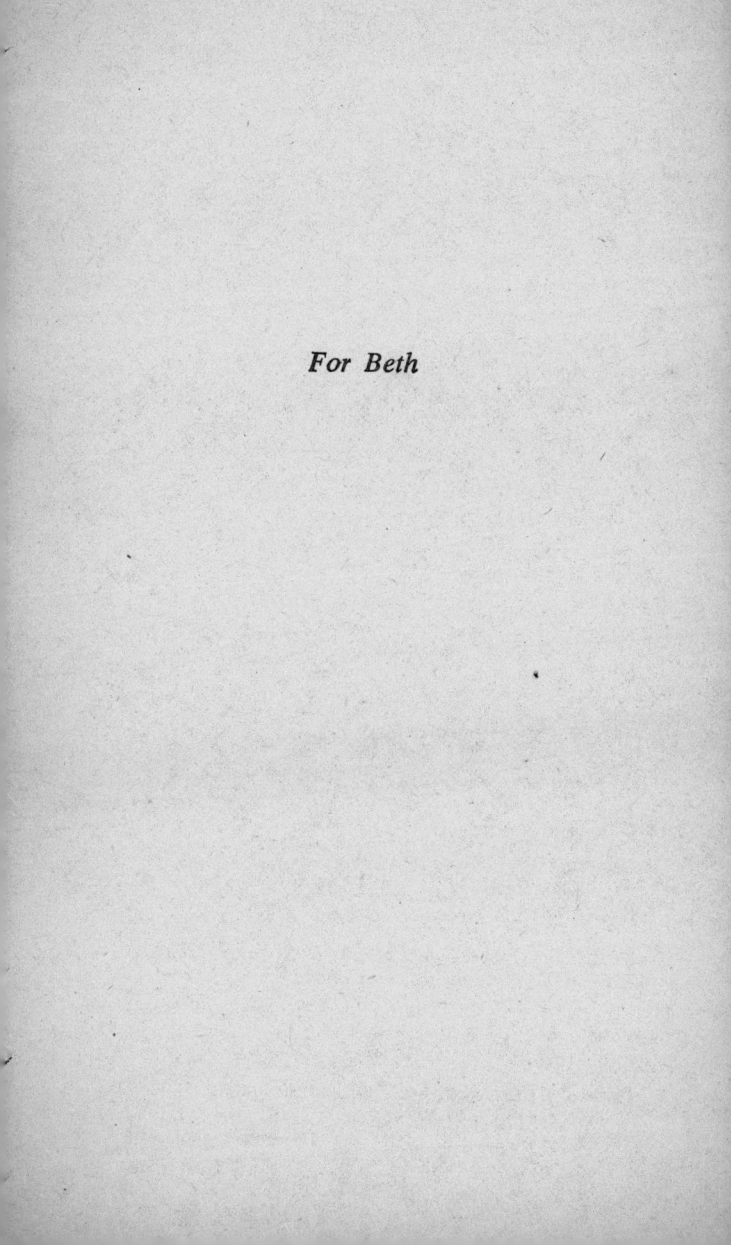

At Bat brings you the stories of four great baseball sluggers:

- Henry Aaron: The Atlanta Braves' superstar who stands one run behind Babe Ruth's homer record—which many thought would stand for another forty years.
- Bobby Murcer: From a kid who almost folded under the crippling pressure to become an instant superstar, he has developed into the standout team leader of the Yankees.
- Johnny Bench: The supercatcher who knocks them out of the park—the great star of the Cincinnati Reds.
- Reggie Jackson: The young superstar of the flamboyant Oakland A's who has overcome his earlier problems as a player.

Here are four of baseball's top players—their lives, hopes, disappointments, failures and triumphs. All outstanding at defense, these men are major threats *At Bat*.

CONTENTS

1 Henry Aaron   1
2 Bobby Murcer   39
3 Johnny Bench   72
4 Reggie Jackson 110

1. Henry Aaron

On the night of June 10, 1972, the Atlanta Braves were in Philadelphia for a game against the hometown Phillies. It was a cool evening, the heat and humidity of summer not yet arrived. Players sat close together in the dugouts, most of them wrapped in warmup jackets to keep out the dampness and chill that was in the air.

It was still early in the season, but it was already obvious that neither team was going anywhere fast. The Phils, in fact, had one of the worst teams in baseball. The Braves, on the other hand, had a power-laden lineup, but little pitching to back it up. They lacked the needed balance to make a serious run at the pennant.

Consequently, there wasn't much of a crowd on hand that night, but it didn't deter the Brave hitters. They went to work and pounded the pill all over the lot. By the sixth inning, Atlanta had a big lead and the Phils had their umpteenth pitcher, a righthander named Wayne Twitchell, in the ballgame.

Once again the Braves opened up, quickly loading the bases. Out of the Atlanta dugout ambled number 44, Henry Aaron. The veteran slugger looked almost unconcerned, detached, as he made his way slowly to the plate, gazing out at Twitchell while he walked.

In the box he settled into his familiar stance, midway right side, left foot slightly closer to the plate. He held his bat high, right elbow extended upward. He was loose and relaxed.

Twitchell took a deep breath. The young pitcher didn't want to get burned any more. He decided he had the strength to blow the ball past Aaron. He wound and delivered. Ball one! Aaron didn't budge. Twitchell threw again. This was a strike, inside corner. Aaron rested the bat on his shoulder until the pitcher was ready. Then it came up again.

For the third time Twitchell threw his fastball. This time Aaron wanted it. He took a short stride, then snapped the bat around, his powerful wrists giving it a sharp whip. Seconds later it was Twitchell who was whipping around, watching the flight of the ball out into left centerfield. It was too late for him to do anything but watch it pass over the fence for a grand slam home run.

Hank Aaron trotted slowly around the bases. He saw the three runners scoring ahead of him, smiled slightly, then came across the plate to grab the congratulating hands that awaited him. Twitchell scuffed at the mound angrily. He had just become an unwilling part of baseball history.

The home run was the 38-year-old Aaron's tenth of the season. But more important, it was the 649th of his long career, and it enabled him to pass 41-year-old Willie Mays and move into sole possession of second place on the all-time list. In addition, it was the 14th grandslammer of his career, and that tied a National League record previously held by the late Gil Hodges.

Why was the home run so significant? Simply because it brought into crystal clear focus an undeniable fact of baseball life. Hammerin' Hank Aaron had an excellent chance of breaking one of the game's most revered records, Babe Ruth's career mark of 714 home runs.

It was a record many thought would stand forever. Even when Roger Maris broke Ruth's single-season mark of 60, by belting 61 in 1961, baseball traditionalists pointed to the enlarged schedule as a reason for Maris' success, and added, "Nobody will ever touch the Babe's career mark."

Many believed that to be true. Then in the middle 1960s, two sluggers—Mickey Mantle and Willie Mays—climbed over the 500 mark. A few years later they were joined by Aaron, and some people began to talk about the trio in terms of their ultimate capabilities.

But Mantle was forced to the sideline by injuries and retired with 536 round trippers to his credit. Mays marched on, driving over the 600 mark, and for the first time there was a legitimate challenger for the Ruthian standard. It was Willie's race against time.

Then, in 1971, people realized it wasn't Willie's race alone. Aaron, too, whacked number 600, and he was chasing Mays. Some three years younger and in seemingly better health than Willie, Hank continued to belt the ball. He slammed 47 homers, a career high, as a 37-year-old in 1971. And when the season ended, he had 639, trailing Mays by just nine home runs.

When Aaron hit his homer off Twitchell that night in Philadelphia, he served notice that he was the only one with a chance. Mays was near the end of the line. He wasn't playing regularly and hadn't hit a single home run in the first two months of the season.

Suddenly all the talk centered around Aaron. Writers and broadcasters began looking at the books. They found that the homer mark wasn't the only one within Aaron's range. The great rightfielder of the Braves was near the top of the all-time list in games played, at-bats, runs scored, hits, total bases, runs batted in and extra base hits.

None of this should have come as a surprise to so many people, but it did. The reason is simple. Henry Aaron is a quiet superstar. He plays the game with skills matched only by a select few. He does his job, day after day, without creating any kind of furor, without verve or flash. Furthermore, he played his entire caretr in Milwaukee, then Atlanta, never having had the benefit of the big-city press, such as is the case in New York, or on the west coast. As a consequence, Aaron's skills and achievements went largely unnoticed for a great number of years.

"I know I'm not flashy," Hank Aaron once said. "But I don't try to be. I just play my natural way. It's almost the same as the way I dress. I have good clothes and dress well, but not flashy. That's just my way and I can't change it."

His easy style of play affected others the same way. Billy Bruton, who was the Braves' centerfielder when Hank came up in 1954, once said, "I used to say a prayer every time Hank went after a fly ball. It always looked as if he'd never get there. But after he was around awhile and I saw the things he could do, I never worried about him again."

And another former teammate, Felipe Alou, who played both with and against Aaron, said this: "I never realized how good Henry was until I played alongside him every day. In the outfield he gives everyone so much of the right field line, yet he gets to every ball hit out there in an easy way."

If Aaron's teammates didn't see his greatness at first, how were the fans and writers supposed to see it? It was a long time before Hank's talents were fully appreciated by the vast majority of baseball people. And by then he was creeping up on a host of all-time records.

Now there is only admiration and respect for this great slugger, a lifetime .300 hitter, fine outfielder and simply marvelous all-around ballplayer. He deserves to be ranked right up there with the best of them and he will be.

Still looking trim at six feet, 180 pounds, Henry Aaron doesn't appear to be a man pushing 40. Only his face is fuller, otherwise he looks much like the shy,

20-year-old youngster who reported to the Braves as a rookie in 1954. And he's proud of the fact that he's been so durable, his only serious injury having been a broken ankle in September of that very first year.

"I take good care of myself," Hank says. "I know I'll only go as far as my body takes me. I always come into spring training at 188 pounds or so and I'm down around 180 when the season begins."

You can't refute the Aaron logic. The results speak for themselves. In 1972, Henry put 34 more home runs to his total of 639. Add that up. The answer is 673. And the difference between 673 and 714 is 41. Barring injury or a sudden decline in his skills, most people feel that Hank Aaron will be baseball's new all-time home run champion sometime during the 1974 season.

As is his style, Henry is not acting overly excited about it. With each passing day, month, year, he's been asked more and more about his chances of setting a new mark. He always answers coolly and rationally.

"Sure, I think about it (the record)," he says. "I think I can do it if I stay healthy and if I have a strong man batting behind me. That way, they can't pitch around me."

Then Hank talked about another phenomenon that's come his way. "I get a lot of letters asking me not to break the record. They're not vicious letters, mind you, but apparently there is so much tradition and sentiment involved with Ruth's record that people don't want to see it broken.

"I guess a lot of people will be disappointed if anyone tops Ruth. But if I do it, I'll fully expect someone else to come along and top me some day."

Henry Aaron has been a realist ever since he came to the majors. But when he was a boy, he had a lot of the dreamer in him, and he needed that quality to get where he is today.

Hank was born in Mobile, Alabama, on February 5,

1934, the third child of Herbert and Estella Aaron. Four other children were to follow, so the Aaron family was a large one.

The Aarons came to Mobile just two years before Henry was born. Before that, they lived in Camden, Alabama, a small farm town near Mobile. Both Mr. and Mrs. Aaron knew what it was like to work all day in the fields and they wanted to improve the lot of their growing family.

So they moved to the Down-the-Bay section of Mobile, where many other poor black families lived. Mr. Aaron was a very hard-working man. He soon got a job as a boilermaker's assistant and made enough money to move his family to a better neighborhood, the Toulminville section of Mobile. That's where young Henry grew up.

As a youngster, Henry was shy and withdrawn. He didn't like playing with the other boys and often stayed very close to home. Even when he was five years old, he had no desire to explore the world. He just liked staying around his mother and playing in the safety of his back yard.

"Henry could spend hours by himself when he was a boy," Mrs. Aaron said. "He used to go out in the yard and play with a top for hours on end, just spinning and watching it. But I'll never forget one day when I walked out there. He was playing with the top as usual, only this time he wasn't spinning it, he was hitting it with a baseball bat."

That was the first indication of Hank's attraction to the game. It was just a few years later, when he was eight, that the youngster saw major league baseball for the first time.

In those days, baseball teams trained in Florida during the spring, then made their way north by train, stopping every day or so to play a game in the cities along the route. That way, the players had additional practice time, and many more people had a chance to get a glimpse of the major league game.

Mobile was a regular stop along the way, and Henry would go out and sit by himself in the bleachers at Hartwell Field, watching some of the great players in action. He saw Musial, Williams, Feller and DiMaggio—and followed their exploits with wonderment. DiMaggio had a special fascination for him. He liked the Yankee Clipper's style and grace, and when he'd come home he'd always announce:

"I'm gonna play ball like Joe DiMaggio when I grow up."

Still, Henry played little ball with the other boys, preferring to throw a ball around with his older brother, Herbert, Jr., or with his Uncle Bubba. But he slowly got over his shyness and started playing more with the other boys. He really loved the game right from the start.

The United States was in the midst of World War II at that time, and for the next three years not many of the top stars came to Mobile. They were all in the service. By the time they returned in 1946, Henry had become an avid fan and good young ballplayer.

"I really can't say where I got my ability from," Hank explained. "My Daddy always worked very hard from the time I knew him, but I heard he was a good ballplayer when he was younger and I guess that's where I got some of it from.

"One thing I know about my father was that he hated laziness. I remember one time it was my turn to chop wood for the fire. I just didn't feel like doing it, so I chopped a small amount, then tried to pile it up so it looked like more. My Daddy didn't go for that. I got a good whipping for that one and learned not to be lazy when Herbert Aaron was around."

The year was 1946 when most of the top baseball stars returned from the war and started playing at Hartwell Field again. And this time Henry had a special reason for going, even if it meant skipping school. The Brooklyn Dodgers had a new player named Jackie Robinson and he was the first black man ever to play with a major league team.

Robinson's presence helped turn the dream into reality. Young Henry watched Jackie's progress during the next several years. He saw other young blacks joining major league teams. Now there was a chance that he could really play like Joe DiMaggio or Jackie Robinson. From that point on he thought of little else.

School really didn't mean much to him. And whenever there was a baseball game around, he skipped. One time, he was sitting in a local poolroom, listening to the Dodgers playing on the radio. Who should walk by? None other than Herbert Aaron. He brought his son home and the two had a long talk.

Hank told his father that he wanted to be a ballplayer. It was the only thing he was interested in.

"You can still be a ballplayer and have your education, too," Mr. Aaron said. He and his wife believed in education for all their children. But Henry had the answer.

"I can't learn much about playing ball in a classroom, can I?" he said.

"Listen," said Mr. Aaron. "I give you fifty cents to take to school with you every day for your lunch and whatever else you need. I take a quarter with me to work. That's because it's worth more to me to see you get an education than it is for me to eat."

It was obvious that Mr. Aaron was thinking of his youngster's welfare and Henry promised to finish high school. But he knew what he wanted and was determined to reach his goal.

By that time, Henry was playing a lot of softball around Mobile, and he was quickly gaining a reputation as the best young hitter around. The odd thing was that he batted crosshanded, with his left hand above his right on the bat. Even so, his wrists were already strong enough for him to whack line drives all over the field.

When he went to Central High, an all-black school in Mobile, he was an instant star. "Henry was the kingpin for two years," says his coach, Edwin Foster. "He was here for two years, and we lost only three games in that time. He was really a great player with us."

Hank was an infielder in those days, playing both second and short. He also played guard on the Central High football team for one year, but gave it up because he didn't want to risk an injury that would hamper his baseball career. Then, before his senior year, his parents decided to send him to the Josephine Allen Institute, a private school in Mobile where they thought he'd have a better chance to get ready for college.

When he was about fifteen and just starting to play at Central, the Dodgers held a tryout camp in Mobile. Henry rushed out with great expectations, but quickly learned a lesson in the law of survival. Every time he made a move to go out on the field or get a turn in the batting cage, a bigger boy pushed him out of the way. He never did get a chance to show his stuff and went home in tears. He realized then that he'd have to be more aggressive if he wanted to be a real ballplayer.

That's how he played the game from then on. One day shortly afterward, he was playing in a sandlot game when a man named Ed Scott approached him. Scott beckoned for Hank to come over after the game.

"How would you like to make some money, Aaron?"

Henry was puzzled. He wondered what Scott had in mind, but when the man added, "Playing baseball," Henry was all ears.

Ed Scott wanted Hank to play for the Mobile Black Bears, one of the best semi-pro teams in the area. The Bears met many of the top Negro League teams that passed through Mobile, and young Hank was excited at the opportunity to play with and against good ballplayers, men much older than himself.

It took some convincing for Mrs. Aaron to go along

with the idea, but she finally consented. Henry played for the Bears some evenings and on Sundays, operating at short and second, and hitting better than anyone.

The Bears' payroll came from the old-fashioned pass-the-hat system, with the fans contributing whatever they could. Players generally got from three to five dollars a game, depending on how well they played. Hank Aaron set records then also. Sometimes he did so well that they gave him ten dollars a game.

For two years, Henry played outstanding ball for the Bears. The older players liked and respected him. Late in the summer of 1951, the Bears scheduled a game with the Indianapolis Clowns, widely regarded as one of the best of the barnstorming Negro League teams in the country.

With many black ballplayers now beginning to filter into the major leagues. Negro League teams were feeling a talent squeeze and were on the lookout for fresh young ballplayers. And Henry Aaron was the best-looking kid they'd seen in a long time.

Against the Clowns that August afternoon, Hammerin' Hank slammed a double and two singles, as well as making a couple of sparkling plays in the field. When the game was over, Bunny Downs, the Clowns' road manager, came looking for Hank.

Downs tossed a bevy of questions at the youngster, asking his age, whether he was still in school, when he graduated, what other positions he played.

To the last question, Henry said, "I'll play any position you want."

"That's what I like to hear," Downs replied. "Henry, how would you like to play baseball for the Indianapolis Clowns?"

Henry was stunned, and he recalls his reaction to this day. "I couldn't believe what the man was saying. But I didn't let him see how excited I was. I just sort of played it real casual and said something like, 'I don't see why not.' So he started telling me that he'd send me a contract as soon as I got out of high school and I could expect to hear from him. One reason I didn't show my excitement was that I didn't know if he was on the level. I figured I'd just wait and see."

Sure enough, right before he graduated from Josephine Allen Institute in June of 1951, Hank received a contract in the mail offering him $200 a month to play baseball for the Clowns.

The only problem was his parents. Mr. and Mrs. Aaron didn't know too much about baseball and didn't really understand what it meant to play professionally. They certainly couldn't imagine their son playing alongside established major league stars. For them, college was the best answer for Henry. He'd had a few scholarship offers, in fact, and they were determined for him to continue his education.

It took some mighty fancy talking for Henry Aaron to convince his parents to let him play for the Clowns. But they saw how serious their son was about baseball and they didn't want to hold him back. So, in May of 1952, Henry got ready to leave home for the first time.

"I was really worried about Henry leaving home," said Mrs. Aaron. "He had never been away before and he hadn't even been around other people much. Now, all of a sudden, he was going out on his own with all these other people. I wasn't sure if he could handle it.

"All I could think of was a little boy, playing by himself in the back yard, or sitting in the house reading comics. I knew he was going to be homesick and I wished he was just a little older. But I knew he had to go. I gave him two dollars, packed up two pairs of pants, and made him two sandwiches. That was all he left home with."

So it was on the train and up to Winston Salem, North Carolina, where the Clowns were training for the upcoming season. Henry joined a team that had some disgruntled, older players. Some were bitter because the color line had been broken in the majors long after they were in their prime, their opportunity to play in the big leagues lost forever. Others were just worried about losing their jobs.

As a consequence, they didn't take to young, talented Hank Aaron with much friendliness. Few talked to him. He had trouble getting the proper equipment. He was alone and not enjoying his first experience in baseball at all.

"Henry was calling us up all the time," said Mrs. Aaron. "He was homesick, just like I knew he'd be. He told us about how the older players were treating him. They were giving him a plain old hard time. He said he didn't even have a warmup jacket. He was alone there and thought maybe he should come home.

"I didn't know what to tell him. In one way, I wanted to tell him to come home, but I knew that wasn't right. He had worked so hard to get there. So I put his brother, Herbert, Jr., on the phone. Herbert was six years older than Henry and I knew Henry would listen to him.

"Herbert told Henry to stay. He reminded him of how badly he wanted to play baseball and that he shouldn't give up his big chance without a fight. Henry agreed, and said he'd stay with the Clowns."

Henry Aaron fought back the best way he knew. He became Hammerin' Hank and began tattooing the baseball. Before long, he was the team's leading hitter and run producer. Now the older players had to respect him.

There was one problem. Amazingly enough, Hank still hit crosshanded. It has to rank as one of baseball's great feats, that this youngster, batting incorrectly, holding the bat in an awkward fashion that prevented him from using all his power, was able to hit so well. Finally, one day, Syd Pollock, the owner of the Clowns, approached him.

"Henry, you're the team's best hitter," he told the

youngster. "But there's no way you'll ever make the majors batting that way. You've got to change."

Never one to ignore good advice, Hank began practicing with the correct grip, and pretty soon he found himself hitting the ball even harder, hanging liners all over the field, and smashing long, towering home runs. But it was a hard habit for him to break. He often found himself reverting to the crosshanded grip with two strikes on him and he had to make a conscious effort not to do it.

But when he finally broke the habit, he hit better than ever. The word about him was spreading. He wasn't with the Clowns three months when he was told that several big league scouts were already making inquiries about him. He reacted to the news with his usual detached air, but inside he was wild with excitement.

The Giants were the first team that expressed a real interest in Hank. But Syd Pollock wrote a letter to the Boston Braves, informing them about the young slugger. The Braves dispatched scout Dewey Griggs to take a look. The Clowns were due in Buffalo, New York, to play a doubleheader against the Kansas City Monarchs. Griggs was there.

To put it mildly, Hank Aaron was hot that day. He came to the plate nine times and banged out seven hits, including two long home runs. In the field, he started five double plays. Griggs's eyes almost popped out of his head.

In order for a major league team to get Henry's services, they had to buy his contract from Syd Pollock. Before long, both the Giants and Braves began to talk with Henry and with Pollock.

The Giants started it. They offered Henry a $300-a-month contract and said they'd send him right to a Class A minor league team. He'd be just a step from the majors and the offer was intriguing to him. But Dewey Griggs scoffed when he heard it.

"They're pikers," he said. "The Braves will pay you $350 a month and we'll start you off with a Class C team. That way, there won't be any pressure on you and you can work your way up at your own pace."

Henry was advised to go with the Braves. They made a little better offer and would send him to an easier club. He'd played with black teams all his life and there would be an amount of adjusting to be done.

When the Braves offered Syd Pollock $10,000 for Henry's contract, the deal was closed. Looking back at the turn of events that made Hank Aaron a Brave, a sportswriter said:

"It's too bad for the Giants that they didn't make a better offer. Could you imagine Hank Aaron and Willie Mays playing on the same team down through the years? What a combination! The whole face of baseball might have been different. With those two in the same lineup, the New York fans couldn't have stayed away from the Polo Grounds. Who knows, the Giants might never have left New York."

It's an interesting possibility, but it never came to pass. Hank signed and was instructed to report to the Braves' Class C team at Eau Claire, Wisconsin. He said goodbye to the rest of the Clowns, got a handshake and a cardboard suitcase from Syd Pollock, and left. In return for the suitcase, Pollock had a $10,000 check from the Braves. So he didn't do badly for having had Aaron just a few short months.

As for Henry, he was another step closer to his dream. It seemed like only yesterday that he had been pleading with his parents for a chance to play with the Clowns, hoping it would lead him to the majors someday. Now, at the age of 18, he was already with the Boston Braves organization. It was all happening so fast.

But dazzled as he was by all that had occurred, he didn't let it affect his performance. At Eau Claire, he was an immediate sensation, his free-swinging style exciting the fans and driving in the runs.

Hank played in 87 games for Eau Claire during the last half of the 1952 season. He batted a solid .336, hit nine homers and had 61 runs batted in. In addition, he stole 25 bases and played a fine game at second base. He was named to the Northern League all-star team and was voted the league's Rookie of the Year. Henry Aaron was on his way.

"That Northern League pitching was really tough," he says now, looking back. "It was by far the toughest brand of ball I'd played up to then. But I was getting older and beginning to have more confidence in my ability than I ever had before."

Henry's greatest season was rewarded. At first, he was told that he'd be headed for the Milwaukee Brewers, the Braves' Triple A farm club. But before the season started, the Braves franchise was moved from Boston to Milwaukee, and the minor league Brewers were shifted to Toledo. At the same time, it was decided that Henry should play for Jacksonville, a Class A team in the South Atlantic or Sally League.

But Henry would have more than baseball to think about during the 1953 season. He and two other blacks were told that they would be breaking the Sally League color line that year. League cities were all located in the so-called deep south and there might be some problems. It didn't really turn out that way. There were a few tense moments, but no real trouble.

Blacks stayed in separate quarters, usually private homes in the Negro sections of town. Ironically, it worked out well, because, as Henry said, the people in the private homes always wanted to do everything to please them. They were proud to be helping ballplayers who might soon be in the major leagues. So Henry and his two teammates had home-cooked meals and comfortable beds. It was usually better quarters than the hotel where the white players stayed.

As for breaking the color line, Hank Aaron had his own approach.

"There was only one way to break the color line," he said, "and that was to play well. If you played good, exciting baseball, most of the people don't remember what color you are."

Hank practiced what he preached. As soon as he stepped into a Jacksonville uniform he started hitting. Insults came out of the stands in one big southern city, but Hank and the others learned to ignore them, no matter how much it hurt. If anything, the slurs prodded Hank to hit even better.

Ben Geraghty was Hank's manager that year and the two grew very close. Geraghty liked and admired the youngster from Mobile and he knew that he had a future star in the making.

"Henry was the most relaxed kid I've ever seen," Geraghty said. "Nothing bothered him. During the long bus rides he'd always fall asleep. He could sleep anywhere.

"And he had a deadpan look about him so I never knew when he was pulling my leg and when he was serious. I remember one time in midseason I decided to change all the signs. Henry came up the next day and I gave him the new take sign. Well, he promptly hit a homer.

"When he got back to the dugout and I asked him why he didn't take the pitch, he told me that I gave him the hit sign. I said no, that was the old hit sign, but the new *take* sign. He just looked at me with that deadpan of his and said, 'Damn, I only got around to learning the signs yesterday.' I settled the issue the easy way. For the rest of the season I just let him hit away."

Henry hit away, all right, to the tune of 208 hits in just 137 games. He belted 22 homers, drove in 125 runs and led the league in hitting with a .362 average. He also topped the Sally League in hits, RBI's, doubles and runs scored. It came as no surprise when he was named the loop's Most Valuable Player by a wide margin.

Something else happened to Hank that year. He met a girl, Barbara Lucas, who was a business student at Florida A & M University. They began dating, fell in love and were married on October 6, 1953. Two days later, the Aarons were off on an unexpected honeymoon. The news came from Ben Geraghty.

"The Braves want to take a long look at your next spring," the jaunty manager said.

Henry felt his heart jump with excitement. Then Geraghty continued:

"They feel you'll have a better chance to make the club as an outfielder. You still have too much to learn about the infield and they feel they're pretty well set there. What they want is for you to play winter ball in Puerto Rico, as an outfielder. What do you say?"

Henry looked at Geraghty with his usual deadpan. "It's fine with me, as long as I don't have to speak Spanish."

Despite his reservations about the language barrier, Henry didn't mind going at all. It was perfect, an extended honeymoon for him and Barbara, plus playing baseball. And best of all, the next spring he'd have his first real chance at making a major league team.

Playing the outfield came easy to him. He wasn't worried at all about his fielding, and as for his hitting, that was as natural as eating a piece of pie. He was officially assigned to the triple A team at Toledo for the 1954 season, but he'd be training with the big club at Bradenton, Florida.

The 1954 Milwaukee Braves were considered a coming team in the National League. They already had some fine performers like pitchers Warren Spahn and Lew Burdette, catcher Del Crandall, outfielder Billy Bruton, infielders John Logan, Eddie Mathews and Joe Adcock. Most of them were still young ballplayers approaching their best playing years.

Two unsettled positions were leftfield and second base. Manager Charlie Grimm and general manager John Quinn engineered two trades that hopefully solved the problem. They acquired second baseman Danny O'Connell from Pittsburgh and outfielder Bobby Thomson from the Giants. Thomson was the hero of the 1951 pennant with his dramatic playoff homer against the Dodgers. When he joined the club, Hank Aaron was sure he'd be spending the summer in Toledo.

Early in the spring, Henry didn't play much. He pinch hit, or pitch ran, not much more. The Braves wanted to work Thompson into their ballclub and he was getting most of the playing time. Young Aaron wasn't really getting a chance to show his stuff.

Then on March 15, fate took a hand. The Braves were playing an exhibition game against the Yankees. Henry made his customary pinch-hitting appearance, had already showered, and was standing under the bleachers drinking a coke and watching the remainder of the ballgame.

Thomson was up and promptly smacked a hard shot down the leftfield line. He dug around first and went sliding into second with a double. Then Henry noticed that Bobby wasn't getting up. He was twisting in pain on the ground. Minutes later he was being carried from the field on a stretcher, his ankle broken.

The next question was, who would take Thomson's place? Everyone tried to guess, but few people even mentioned Hank Aaron. Most of the newspaper people still didn't know him. But the day after Thomson's injury, manager Grimm walked slowly toward Henry in the clubhouse. Suddenly, he picked up the youngster's glove and tossed it to him.

"Here, kid," the old manager said. "You're my new leftfielder. The job's yours until someone takes it away from you."

Twenty-year-old Hank Aaron stood there open-mouthed. It was the last thing he expected to happen.

He figured veteran Jim Pendleton would get the first shot and he'd be on his way back to the minors. But he wasn't complaining. Then, before the start of the regular season, general manager Quinn made it official. He told Henry that the Braves had purchased his contract from Toledo.

"I was so happy to be in the big leagues that I just signed the contract Mr. Quinn put in front of me," Henry said. "I didn't even know what my salary was. But I trusted Mr. Quinn and figured he'd take care of all the details."

Hank went hitless in his first major league game against Cincinnati. He was nervous and excited. He knew it would take him awhile to get used to the majors. But he felt better when he learned how much confidence manager Grimm had in him.

"Henry's not the spectacular type," Grimm told reporters. "He makes everything look easy out there. So we're not going to try to make another Willie Mays out of him. But mark my words, he'll be around long after Willie's gone."

The encouragement must have helped. On April 23, Hank blasted his first big league homer off veteran Vic Raschi of St. Louis. Two days later he whacked another, this time off crafty Stu Miller. Now he was sure he could hit major league pitching, and hit it with power.

From that point on, Hank was an everyday player, continuing to hit well and patrolling the outfield more than adequately. What's more, the Braves were in a pennant race, battling the Dodgers and Giants for the flag, so the youngster from Mobile was playing the game under pennant pressure and producing in the clutch.

On September 5, the Braves were just five games from the top and still considered to have a chance at winning it all. The team was in Cincinnati for a doubleheader. In the first game, Grimm decided to rest his rookie and started the recovered Bobby Thomson in left.

Thomson got a hit in the seventh inning and Henry went in to run for him. Later in the game, Aaron batted on his own and doubled. He started the second game and stroked hits his first three times up. Then he came up again late in the game.

Henry felt good that day, relaxed and loose. He felt as if no man alive could throw the ball past him. Once again he picked out a fastball, whipped his wrists around, and sent a long drive sailing over the centerfielder's head. He turned on the speed, rounding first, then second. As he approached third, he saw the coach signaling for him to slide and he hit the dirt. Safe!

It was his fifth straight hit of the afternoon. But something was wrong. His right ankle was paining him. He tried to get up, but couldn't. Everyone gathered around and he was helped off the field. Irony had struck again. It was a broken ankle (Thomson's) that got him into the lineup, and now a broken ankle (his own) would take him out. Doctors operated and put a pin in the ankle, then told him to take the rest of the year off.

So Henry sat on the sidelines and watched his team finish third to the Giants and Dodgers. But he had certainly produced in his rookie season. He played in 122 games, collected 131 hits, belted 13 homers, and drove home 69 runs. His batting average was a solid .280. One sportswriter, in fact, noted just how solid it was.

"Some .280 hitters get there by batting .450 against the worst pitchers in the league and doing next to nothing against the good ones," the man said. "Then there are the tough .280 hitters, men like Tommy Henrich and Pee Wee Reese, who get important hits against the important pitchers and tough teams. And that's just what Aaron did in his rookie season."

It was quite a compliment to the young star, but Hank himself wasn't quite satisfied.

"I'm happy I got a chance to play in the big leagues," he said, "but I feel I should have done better on the field."

Then someone reminded him of the year he had, adding that he had done better than many baseball greats in their first years. Players like Ty Cobb, Rogers Hornsby and Willie Mays hadn't hit as well as Henry in their rookie seasons.

"Maybe," Henry replied. "But I look at it this way. I've been hitting .340 all my life. I was hitting well over .400 with the Indianapolis Clowns. So hitting .280 with the Braves doesn't make me feel as if I've done my best."

When Hank reported to the Braves training camp the next year, his ankle was completely healed. And there was a surprise waiting for him. Hanging in his locker was uniform number "44." He had worn the number "5" his rookie year, but expressed a liking for double numbers, and the club decided to make the young slugger happy. He was now "44," and he'd wear that number for a long time.

Henry really began to find the range in 1955. Playing in all but one game, he pounded out 189 hits, slammed 27 homers, and drove in 106 runs. He also led the league in doubles with 37 and batted over .300 for the first time at .314. And at midseason he had participated in his first all-star game, held at Milwaukee that year. He thrilled the home fans with two singles in two trips, driving home one run. And he has played in the mid-summer classic every year since.

There was one thing that dampened the 1955 season. The Braves finished second to the Dodgers in the National League race. Reporting to spring training before the 1956 season, Henry and his teammates were determined to take the pennant.

A newsman tells a funny story about Hank in 1956.

It's said that he reported to spring training that year, pulled on an old uniform, borrowed a bat from someone and stepped into the cage for his first swings. He went after the first three pitches and drove each one into the distant stands.

Seeing that, he yawned, stepped out of the box, discarded the bat and drawled, "Ol' Hank is ready."

Well, "Ol' Hank" was all of 22 years old then, although he conserved his energy like a man of 40.

The 1956 season turned into one of frustration for all the Braves. When it was over, Milwaukee had held the lead for 126 days, the Dodgers for just 17. But the Brooklyn team held it when it counted, on the last day of the season, and the Braves were second-best once again. Even the Milwaukee owners were running out of patience. Toward the end of the year they fired Charlie Grimm and replaced him with tough Fred Haney. They wanted it all in '57, and wanted it badly.

Hammerin' Hank had another fine year in 1956, leading the league in hitting with a .328 mark, stroking 26 homers, and driving home 92 runs. He also topped the N.L. in hits with 200, doubles with 34, and total bases with 340. He was the real thing, all right, and quickly becoming a star.

Since the Braves moved from Boston to Milwaukee in 1954, the city had been on a baseball bender. The fans whirled through the turnstiles in County Stadium at a breakneck pace, more than two million paying their way into the park during 1956. And they watched exciting baseball. Aside from Aaron, the team had a pair of 20-game winners in Spahn and Burdette, more slugging from Ed Mathews and Joe Adcock, and played a generally superior brand of ball. Only no pennant.

In fact, Hank himself admitted after the 1956 season that for the first time in his life it really hurt him to lose.

Everyone on the team worked hard in spring training. It seemed to pay. Milwaukee won nine of its first 10 games in 1957 and jumped out in front. But a slump caught the team off guard and by mid-June dictated some changes. The result was a trade that brought veteran second baseman Red Schoendienst to the Braves from the Giants.

Schoendienst gave the team its final link. A switch-hitting leader, the Redhead was a smooth fielder and tough hitter from either side of the plate. When he came to the Braves, manager Haney put him in the second spot in the lineup. The incumbent second hitter was moved into the fourth spot. His name: Hank Aaron.

The addition of Schoendienst and shifting of Hank to the cleanup spot proved an elixir for the team. They began winning again and surged back into first place. Later in the season centerfielder Bruton was hurt. Haney asked Hank if he'd mind moving to center. The youngster said he'd give it a try, and made the switch without difficulty. He was a versatile, all-around player.

Milwaukee kept getting closer and closer. On the night of September 23, 1957, the Braves were playing the Cardinals with a chance to clinch the pennant. The game was tied after nine, and was still tied when Henry came to bat in the 11th inning. He was facing a pitcher named Billy Muffet and there was one man on base.

As usual, Henry looked relaxed at the plate. But when he got a pitch he liked, he whipped his bat around and sent a towering drive out toward center. It kept carrying deeper and deeper and finally sailed out of the park for a home run. The Braves had won the National League pennant. Henry was hoisted onto the shoulders of his teammates and paraded around the field for the screaming, cheering fans. The entire city erupted in a frenetic celebration. And Hank Aaron called it the happiest moment of his life.

He had put together his first truly super season, leading the National League in homers with 44 and RBI's with 132. His .322 batting average was also near the top of the league. When the ballots were counted after the season, Hammerin' Hank Aaron was voted the National League's Most Valuable Player. In his quiet, unassuming way, he had become a superstar.

Once the pennant celebration died down, the Braves realized they still had a World Series facing them. And they'd be meeting the powerful Yankees of New York, the tough Bronx Bombers who had a habit of spending early October beating National League opponents into submission.

The Yankee roster read like a Who's Who of baseball. Mickey Mantle, Yogi Berra, Whitey Ford, and right on down the line. They were all top ballplayers. Many people felt the Braves couldn't handle the pressure.

Ford opened the series against Warren Spahn in a battle of lefthanders. It was a warm, October afternoon at Yankee Stadium and 23-year-old Hank Aaron looked up at the crowd of 70,000 fans. He found it hard to believe that he was really there, in New York's Yankee Stadium playing in the World Series.

Neither team scored in the first four innings. A double by the Yanks' Hank Bauer got a run home in the fifth. The Bombers then pushed across two more in the sixth and led, 3-0.

The Braves finally got something going in the seventh, putting two men on with none out. And they had Henry Aaron coming up. Most Milwaukee fans thought Haney would have his star bunting. But he didn't.

Ford worked Henry for a two-strike count. Then the cagey southpaw bent a sharp curve over the outside corner. It was a called third strike. The Brave rally was nipped and the Yanks went on to win the first game, 3-1.

Later, manager Haney was asked why he didn't have Hank bunt.

"Listen," he growled, "I don't bunt, especially away from home and with my best hitter up."

It showed how much faith Haney had in his star,

but it didn't win the ballgame. For the second game, Haney named his righthanded ace, Lew Burdette, to oppose the Yankees' Bobby Shantz.

Hank came up to lead off the second inning. He went after a low fastball and hit a long smash to center. Mantle stood in his tracks for a second, not sure where the ball was going to come down. When he realized it was sailing, he started back, but couldn't reach it. Aaron was standing on third by the time Mantle returned the ball to the infield. A single by Adcock brought him home and the Braves led, 1-0.

The Yanks tied it in the second, but after that it was all Milwaukee, as the Braves went on to win, 4-2, with Burdette outstanding on the mound. Now the team looked forward to game three at Milwaukee.

Unfortunately, the homecoming in Milwaukee proved to be a disaster. The Brave pitchers were wild, walking 11 Yankees during the course of the game. The New Yorkers scored three runs in the first inning, two in the third, and two more in the fourth. It was a 7-1 game when Hank came up with one man on base in the fifth.

He was facing big righthander Don Larsen. Hank waited patiently. Larsen threw a fastball and he snapped his strong wrists. The ball flew off his bat, a high, deep drive to left. He watched it drop into the stands for his first World Series homer. It felt good, but the Yanks still led, 7-3.

When the Bombers erupted for five more in the seventh, it was over, a big, 12-3, victory, and a 2-1 Yankee lead in the series. Now the Braves *had* to win game four.

The Yanks took a 1-0 lead in the first inning of that encounter and it began to look bleak. But in the fourth, the Braves got moving. Shortstop Johnny Logan walked, followed by an Ed Mathews double to right. With runners on second and third, Henry stepped in, facing Yankee righthander Tom Sturdivant. The righty threw his favorite pitch, the knuckleball, but Henry was ready. He slammed the flutter pitch into the left-field seats for another home run, putting the Braves in front, 3-1. The big man had come through again.

But the Yanks weren't finished. An Elston Howard home run tied the game in the ninth, and they pushed across a run in the 10th to lead it, 5-4. Then Eddie Mathews saved the Braves with a dramatic 10th-inning homer to give Milwaukee a 7-5 victory and tie the series once more.

The fifth game was an epic pitchers' battle, Burdette squaring off against Ford. Both hurlers were great and neither team could score in the early innings. Then in the last of the sixth, Mathews got an infield hit with two out. Henry wanted to keep the rally going. He swung lightly at an outside curve and blooped a single to right. When Joe Adcock singled to center, the Braves had a run. Burdette made it stand up. Milwaukee won, 1-0, and had a 3-2 lead in the series.

It was back to New York for game six. With another capacity crowd at the Stadium, the Yanks held a 2-1 lead going into the seventh inning. Henry led it off against Bullet Bob Turley. As usual, Turley fired a fastball, and Henry hit it out twice as fast as it had come in. All the way out. It was his third homer and it tied the ballgame.

But once again the hit was wasted. Hank Bauer blasted one for the Bombers in the same inning and the Yanks held on to win, 3-2. The series was tied again, and now it was a winner-take-all, one-game proposition. It would be Burdette pitching for the third time, and facing Don Larsen of the Yankees.

In the third inning, the Braves broke the ice. A two-run double by Mathews chased Larsen, and Aaron greeted reliever Bobby Shantz with a base hit to score Mathews. Another single and subsequent ground out brought Henry home with run number four.

Henry jumped on home plate with both feet. He knew

the Yanks would not catch them now, and he was right. Catcher Del Crandall belted a homer in the eighth and Burdette pitched his second straight shutout as the Braves won, 5-0. They were champions of the baseball world.

Lew Burdette was the Braves' pitching star, and the best hitter in the series was Henry Aaron. He had shown the baseball world that he was a real star. With the pressure on, Hammerin' Hank had 11 hits in seven games, just one short of the series record. He batted .393, and led both teams with three homers and seven runs batted in. It was the highspot of his career thus far.

By that time, Hank Aaron had become one of the most feared hitters in the National League. And the pitchers' suggestions on how to handle him ranged from the ridiculous to the sublime.

One veteran N.L. pitcher, who preferred to remain anonymous, said, "Aaron doesn't swing at his pitch, he swings at *our* pitch. He'll hit anything you throw at him."

Pirate star Vern Law confirmed that diagnosis. "Yeah, that's right," said Law. "My manager suggested I start him with a knuckleball, a pitch I only use after I've set a hitter up for it. So I started Hank with a knuckleball, and he quickly started the scoring with a home run."

Don Newcombe, the veteran ace of the Dodgers, had a better idea. "How do I pitch Aaron?" repeated big Newk. "I'll tell you, I wish I could throw the ball under the plate!"

And the Giants' Sal "The Barber" Maglie had a more direct approach, one which most pitchers would be hesitant to admit. "The only way I could work Aaron," said Sal, "would be to get his face in the dirt. Then he might be edgy and I could try to finesse him. Not always, but sometimes. But the new knockdown rule is helping a hitter like him." That rule provided for an automatic $50 fine for any pitcher throwing the brushback or knockdown deliberately. It took away one of The Barber's favorite weapons.

In other words, Henry was a free swinger with extraordinary bat control. He had no pattern to his hitting. Pitchers could never tell what he would do, what pitches he would take, which ones he'd go after. He had an unusually small number of walks each season, especially for a slugger, and that, too, attested to his fondness for swinging the bat.

Some baseball purists criticized Henry for not taking more walks from overly cautious pitchers trying to work around him. With characteristic nonchalance, Hank threw off the criticism with a quick phrase. "I'd rather hit," he said, shrugging his shoulders.

Hit he did, to the tune of a .326 average in 1958, as the Braves took their second straight pennant. Once again they faced the Yanks in the series. The Braves won the first game, 4-3, as Henry had the tying double in the eighth. He had two more hits as the Braves won the second game, 13.5.

But the Yanks won the third, 4-0, before the Braves came back behind Spahn to win the fourth, 3-0. Hank had two more hits in that one and Milwaukee led, three games to one. It looked as if they'd repeat as champs.

Only this time the team lacked the knockout punch. Bob Turley shut out the Braves in game five, 7-0, and the Yanks took the sixth one in 10 innings, 4-3. It was a one-game series again, with a rematch of Lew Burdette and Don Larsen. Neither was around at the end, the Yanks winning it, 6-2, with Turley the pitching star in relief.

It was a great comeback win for the Yankees and a bitter disappointment for the Braves. Henry had nine hits for a .333 average, but he didn't hit the long ball, with no homers and just two RBI's. It was one of the few times he wasn't the dominant man with the stick.

The next year saw the beginning of the end of the

Milwaukee dynasty. The team fought all year long, but was tied by the Dodgers at the end. In a playoff for the pennant, the Los Angeles team won in two straight games and Milwaukee was finished. A disgruntled Aaron said sadly:

"We lost on the last day of the season in 1956," he said, "and in a playoff in 1959. With a little more luck, we could have won four straight pennants."

Henry was truly a team player. He was saddened by the team's playoff loss. Completely ignored was his own personal season, by far the best since he had come into the league.

He came out of the gate swinging as usual, only this time he was making better contact than ever. By mid-May, the time when most players' averages begin to level off, Henry was still belting the ball at a .468 clip. It made everyone in baseball stop and take notice.

One writer said that it was Aaron, not Mays or Mantle, who was now the logical successor to Stan Musial and Ted Williams as the next great hitter in baseball. And the great Hall of Famer, Rogers Hornsby, claimed that Aaron was the only major leaguer with a reasonable chance to hit .400.

"With those wrists," said the Rajah, "Aaron can be fooled a little and still hit the hell out of the ball."

Hank's manager, Fred Haney, agreed. "Henry is capable of hitting .400, but don't forget, it takes luck as well as ability. The hits have to drop in all year long."

"There are other factors, too," he continued. "In my day, we played at the same time, day in and day out. There were no night games, of course. We ate more regularly and we had easier trips. We didn't have to go cross country all the time.

"Today, a ballplayer might play a tough night game and have to be out on the field the next afternoon, ready to go again. The next day's pitcher can go home early during a night game, but the hitters have to hang around. I think the irregularity of the game hurts the hitter, and that's one of the biggest reasons that it's tougher to hit .400 now."

But for the first time in his career, Henry was badgered by reporters, asking the same questions over and over.

"Can you hit .400, Hank?"

"Do you think you'll crack .400?"

"How's .400 looking, Henry?"

He had to work to develop a defense mechanism. Sometimes he was blunt. One reporter asked about .400 and Hank said, "I don't like to talk about that." Another asked him about his immediate hitting goal, hoping to get into a discussion of a .400 season. But he replied, "Right now I want two more hits. That'll give me 1,000 and I'll be just 2,000 behind Musial."

So Hammerin' Hank was fighting the pressures. It's hard to say whether that got to him or whether it was the intangibles of the long season that Fred Haney mentioned, but his average gradually dropped below .400. Yet he avoided any kind of prolonged slump. It's just that there was such great expectation from the start he had that many people voiced disappointment when .400 seemed no longer probable.

It didn't affect Henry's basic, relaxed style. Someone asked the veteran Philly star, Robin Roberts, about pitching to a hot Aaron and Robin replied, "How can you fool Aaron? He falls asleep between pitches."

It wasn't really that way. Henry himself admitted that he forced himself to relax at the plate. "I'm as tense as the next guy, but you can't hit if you're tight. I make myself relax up there, concentrate on it. I'm not always as casual as most people think. It takes practice to relax."

The 1959 season ended with the playoff loss to the Dodgers. But Henry had done his best. He led the league in hitting for the second time with an eye-popping .355 average. In addition, he topped the N.L. in hits with 223 and in total bases with 400. And his 39 home runs and 123 RBI's weren't totals compiled by a nickel-and-dime hitter. Henry Aaron was simply devastating.

Henry might not have realized it at the time, but he was carrying a bigger load than ever before. The Brave players who had been in their prime when Henry first came up were now becoming aging veterans, who didn't produce at the same high level that they once had. It was a fact of baseball life. The team was moving into a period of decline.

During the next three seasons, Henry continued to play great, all-around baseball. He hit 40, 34 and 45 home runs, driving in 126, 120 and 128 runs during that time. He was under .300 in 1960 (.292), but bounced back for .327 and .323 marks the next two years. Henry was still tops, but the Braves weren't.

The team even had a new manager, Bobby Bragan, a cagey baseball veteran who liked to get the most out of his players. When he talked to Henry, there wasn't much he could criticize, but he did see one area for improvement.

"You're a complete ballplayer," he told the superstar. "But you're not using all your talents. I think you should run the bases more."

When the Braves won the pennant in 1957, the year Henry was the league's Most Valuable Player, he had only stolen one base. With Bragan at the helm starting in 1960, he swiped 16, 21 and 15 over the next three seasons. As usual, when Henry decided to do something on a baseball field, he was quite adept at it. The Braves still had a slugging team, so Henry didn't run all that much. But when he did, he was as good as they come.

In 1963, Hank was the National League's Player of the Year. He had another fantastic all-around season. During that year he became just the fifth man in baseball history to hit more than 30 homers (he had 44) and steal more than 30 bases (he stole 31) in the same season. He led the league in homers again as well as in RBI's with 130 and hits with 201, and also in total bases. His batting average was .319. It was already his tenth season in the big leagues.

The next two seasons were not great ones by Henry's usual standards. He hit .328 and .318, but his run production was off somewhat. Nevertheless, he was still one of the few bright spots on the Braves. The great following in Milwaukee was built around the personalities of the ballplayers. Spahn, Burdette, Mathews, Adcock, Logan, Crandall, Covington. Now they were all fading, or already gone. Players were coming and going, and so were managers. The team was losing its personality and the fans were losing the desire to attend the games.

It was a sad situation, because for almost a decade, Milwaukee had been the hottest baseball town in the country. Now the seats were increasingly empty and the team owners decided they had to do something about it. After the 1965 season, it was announced that the team would be moving to Atlanta, Georgia. The move was greeted with mixed emotions by some of the players. The Braves would be the first big league team to play in the south. Some worried about the treatment the black players would receive.

As it turned out, there was no problem. Henry liked the new ballpark. The ball seemed to carry there, and in his first season he promptly walloped 44 homers and drove in 127 runs. But his batting average was a career low .279.

"I don't really know what happened," he said. "I guess I wanted to hit the long ball for the new fans. I know I'm not a .279 hitter. I'll have the average back up next year."

The low average bothered Henry more than anything else. He did reach a couple of milestones that year. On April 20, he hit the 400th homer of his career off Bo

Belinsky of Philadelphia. And later in the year, he and teammate Eddie Mathews set a record for the most home runs hit by two players on the same team. They would hit 863 before Mathews was traded, and the men who held the record before the two Braves were a couple of guys named Ruth and Gehrig.

To show their appreciation for his long contributions to the team, the Braves awarded Hank a two-year contract prior to the 1967, calling for $100,000 per season. It was about time. Other superstars were making that much, and Henry Aaron was certainly as good as any of them. In addition, he was an immediate favorite with the Atlanta fans. They cheered loud and long every time he came to the plate. And he responded with some very candid comments about his baseball past.

"I guess you could say I was a lost cause in Milwaukee," he admitted. "I was always in the shadows of Burdette, Spahn and Mathews. They were the big boys, even after that big year I had in '57."

So Henry was glad to be in Atlanta. He made good on his promise to get over the .300 mark by hitting .307 in 1967. He still found time to belt another 39 homers and drive in 109 runs. He was as consistent as the sun. The next year, he belted number 500 off Mike McCormick of the Giants. Now he was entering a class reserved for the likes of Mays and Mantle. And he was enjoying every minute of it. At the age of 34, he was finding a second childhood in Atlanta.

"I can't remember getting an ovation like that one when I hit my 500th homer," he said. "And I'm glad I got it off a pitcher like McCormick. It always makes it nicer when you do something like that off one of the best."

Some of the other so-called best also had things to say about Hank Aaron, all of it full of respect and admiration.

Said Sandy Koufax, the great flame-throwing left-hander of the Dodgers, "He's the toughest in the league. There's no way you can pitch him when he's hot."

Giants' star hurler Juan Marichal said it another way after Henry ripped him for four hits and two stolen bases. "That man," said Juan, "if he doesn't beat you one way, he beats you another."

And a journeyman catcher named Charlie Lau, who had played in both leagues, complimented Henry this way:

"I've seen every superstar of recent years—Mantle, Mays, Kaline, Mathews, Clement, all of them—and Aaron's the best. He beats you hitting, running, fielding and stealing. There's nothing he can't do."

Even the great Mickey Mantle looked upon Henry as a very special breed of ballplayer. "As far as I'm concerned," said the Mick, "Henry Aaron is the best ballplayer of my era. He is to baseball of the last 15 years what Joe DiMaggio was before him."

Quite a tribute from a man who always outshone Hammerin' Hank in the public eye. But Henry was finally getting his due. As the records began to fall, reporters and newsmen began approaching him with increased regularity, asking him about this mark and that record. To them, Henry would reply:

"Setting records means you're getting old."

The Braves were aware of his age, too. Although Hank had been in remarkably good health, the team didn't want to take any chances. They began resting him during one game of doubleheaders, and letting him sit out a few day games that followed night games. He also played some first base to save his legs, taking to the new position with his usual style and grace.

For the past several seasons, the Braves' big problem had been pitching. The team always seemed to have enough lumber, but not enough arms. In 1969, they got the right combination going to take the National League's Western Division title. Under the new divisional setup, they had to meet the Eastern Division winner, the New York Mets, to get into the World Series.

Henry made his usual contribution, batting an even .300, belting 44 more homers, and driving in 97 runs. He played in 147 games, indicating how the Braves were resting him.

Atlanta was highly optimistic going into the playoffs, but 1969 was the year of the Mets and nothing was about to stop the New Yorkers. They took three straight from the Braves, despite a home run by Hank Aaron in each game. He did his best to avert defeat, but the Met steamroller was just too much.

In 1970, Henry reached another milestone. He collected his 3,000th base hit, becoming just the ninth man in baseball history to do it. After the game, he told reporters:

"That's what I've always wanted. Now that I have 3,000 hits, everything else will fall into place—the homers, runs batted in, everything. This has meant a lot to me."

Now, more than ever before, people wanted to know about Hank Aaron. While Mays' and Mantle's every move had been relayed to the public for two decades, Henry still toiled in relative obscurity. *The Quiet Legend, The Neglected Superstar, The Quiet Slugger:* these were some of the ways people had referred to Henry over the years. Now, with records falling like trees in a lumber camp, people wanted to know more.

Someone once asked a team official why Henry wasn't more of a holler guy on the field.

"Henry might not be the big back-slapper and talker," the man said, "but he's the real head around here. Everyone on the team has tremendous respect for him. But he's so quiet and so modest that you've got to watch him closely for a long while before you fully realize what a deep influence he has.

"The young players are always watching Henry. They scrutinize his every move, how he swings, how he reacts to different pitchers, how he moves. And he's never too busy to answer any questions they have about all phases of the game and about their personal problems as well.

"And Henry's a good listener. He's always ready to laugh at a joke, making a young guy feel wanted. He creates a whole kind of family mood around here and it's especially valuable when the team isn't going too well. He's a take-charge guy with deeds rather than words, a leader by example."

Henry himself was also beginning to reveal more in his interviews with the press. Early in his career he was very restrained, almost distrustful of reporters. But now, with his status as baseball's elder statesman, he feels he can speak his piece on a variety of topics.

He talked about matters directly related to the game. "An intelligent player is always thinking on the field. Even in the outfield, I watch everything. For instance, on a 3-2 pitch, I'll assume a guy like Nash is going to try to slip a fastball by a hitter like Doug Rader. So I'll edge over to the line a bit, guessing that Doug will go with the pitch late to rightfield."

Ten years earlier, some people thought that Aaron was so relaxed in the outfield that he just ambled around between pitches. They never realized the subtle position changes he was making.

He also talked about baseball-related topics, such as the need for a black manager in the majors. "I think I know enough about the game and about how to get along with a whole team to produce a winner," he said. "So do Ernie (Banks) and Willie (Mays). Unfortunately, no owner has yet had the common sense to hire a black manager. I don't even call it guts, I call it common sense. It's already been proven in baseball that a black man can produce a winner and bring in sellout crowds.

"Now there are certain white managers, guys like Alston and Hodges, who should be hired and rehired, because they've proved they can work with players and they know how to get the most out of a team. But then there's another group of guys who have failed here and failed there. Yet they keep getting rehired by other clubs. It just doesn't seem right."

Back on the ballfield, Henry was still a potent force. At 37, he put together one of the most remarkable seasons ever for a man of his age. On April 27, 1971, Henry stood at home plate facing wily Gaylord Perry of the Giants.

Perry has always been known as a man who might load the baseball. Whether he threw the illegal spitter or not was immaterial. Whatever he threw, Henry hit it hard. The ball sailed deep to left and cleared the wall. It was the 600th home run of his career. He continued to powder the ball the rest of the year. The Braves weren't really going anywhere, but Henry still got himself up for the game day after day.

When the season ended, Henry had played in 139 games, the fewest since his rookie year of 1954. But his 162 hits were good for a .327 batting average. He finished the year with 639 homers, just seven behind Mays, who was three years older at 40 and seemingly near the end of the line.

Despite the publicity and talk of Henry's assault on the Babe, the Atlanta slugger continued to live a quiet private life. He and his wife have a modest home in Atlanta and spend quite a bit of time enjoying their four children.

Shortly before the start of the 1972 season, the Braves announced that Henry Aaron had signed a contract calling for $200,000 per year. It made him the highest paid player in baseball history. After years of playing in shadows, Henry Aaron was finally getting his due.

"He deserves every penny of it," proclaimed Braves' president Bill Bartholomay.

He was right. More and more people will be coming

out to watch Hank Aaron as he begins his final countdown. He showed little signs of slipping in 1972, although his totals were below his outstanding 1971 season. But he still managed 34 homers while playing in just 129 games. He was being rested more and more. Among his 119 hits were 77 RBI's, putting him into second place on the all-time list behind Babe Ruth. His 231 total bases enabled him to pass Stan Musial and become the all-time leader in that department. And his total of 673 homers left him just 41 behind the Babe.

The only area in which he slipped was batting average, coming in with a .265 mark, well below his .312 lifetime figure. He said his days as a .300 hitter were over.

But sometimes Hank Aaron fooled even himself. His drive and sense of self pride give his talents an extra dimension. In 1973, he fooled all of the experts by belting homers at his earlier clip right from the outset of the season. He hit the 700 mark shortly after the all-star break and began closing in on the Babe.

As the second half of the season wound down, Hank's batting average started climbing from the low 200's where it had been all year. With just six games remaining he powered number 712 off Dave Roberts of Houston, his 38th round tripper of the year. Then with two games left he cracked number 713 off Jerry Ruess, also of the Astros.

The final two games were tension-packed. The pitchers were determined not to give up the record-making homers, so they were careful. Amazingly enough, Hank banged out three hits in each contest, and although he didn't get the tying homer, he raised his batting average to .301, hitting an unreal .398 during the second half of the year. He also finished with 40 homers and 96 RBI's to complete his remarkable season.

When Hank popped out in his final at bat, the crowd at Atlanta Stadium gave him a three-minute standing ovation. They were watching a man who was at or near the top in almost every major all-time offensive category. And he'd be back next year to put the icing on the cake.

Some years ago, someone asked him how he'd like to be remembered. Without hesitating, he replied, "I don't want to be anything special or anyone special. I just want to be remembered as plain Henry Aaron."

Well, for once in his life, he was wrong. There's no way that he'll be remembered as plain Henry Aaron. No matter how you cut the pie, Henry Louis Aaron is special. He is very special indeed.

2. Bobby Murcer

Being a Yankee has never been easy for Bobby Murcer. The reason is totally unrelated to Bobby's talents as a ballplayer. It has to do with tradition, New York Yankee tradition, and the quirk of fate that put Bobby Murcer in pinstripes at a particular point in Yankee history.

Bobby came to the Yanks for good in 1969. Coincidentally, that was also the first year in the past 49 that the Bomber attack was missing one of its most treasured trademarks. There was no reigning superstar. And the word superstar has been synonymous with the Yankees ever since the immortal Babe Ruth first donned the New York colors in 1920.

Then in 1925, the Babe was joined by Lou Gehrig, and the two sluggers made their own special mayhem until the Babe left in 1934. Gehrig continued to bust fences until stopped by illness in 1939. By that time, a youngster named Joe DiMaggio was already in his fourth year with the club and was fast becoming the next great superplayer.

DiMag led the Yankee dynasty through the 1951 season, when he announced his retirement. And with typical Yankee magic, that was the same year the team came up with a rookie named Mickey Mantle. The bloodline continued with the famed Switcher until 1968, when Mickey decided his battered legs could take the pounding no longer. He went to spring training in 1969, but then abruptly quit.

Suddenly, there was a look of desperation in the eyes of Yankee rooters. Ruth . . . Gehrig . . . DiMaggio . . . Mantle. They had followed each other in such a neat, orderly fashion that most people thought it was preordained. Shouldn't the next Yankee superslugger have been signed, sealed and delivered when Mickey was ready to call it a career?

But where was he? Maybe it was Joe Pepitone, or Tom Tresh. But they had been around a few years already and were settling into the comfortable position of ballplayers who never reached their original potential. They just weren't superstars. The eyes continued to search.

Then someone spotted a youngster in camp, looked at the roster, and found the name Bobby Murcer. A check of the records revealed some interesting facts. Murcer was from Oklahoma, just like Mickey. And he had been signed by Tom Greenwade, the same scout who inked Mantle. This had to be the guy, the next great Yankee superstar.

The word was out. The papers picked it up, the fans jumped on the bandwagon, and people talked about it wherever Bobby went. Right away, the youngster would be playing in shadows. There were shoes to be filled, big shoes, traditional shoes, shoes that had been worn proudly for half a century. It was a huge burden for any person to bear.

Bobby had been up with the Yanks before, in 1965

and 1966. He had brief trials each time and hadn't been able to put together his hitting and fielding. He was expected to stick in '67 when he received his greetings from Uncle Sam. So the army cost him another two years. By 1969, he was back and ready.

Only the timing was bad. Mantle had just retired and Yankee fans were anxious for another hero. They wanted one right away. And for a while, Bobby seemed to be their man.

Though not a massive slugger in the traditional sense, the 5-11, 180-pound Murcer had a sweet stroke from the left side of the plate. He choked up on the bat slightly, yet the ball jumped when he connected. During spring training, he sprayed sharp line drives all over the lot. He seemed calm and collected. Nothing bothered him. Murcer looked like a hitter all the way.

When the reporters started coming around, their questions were obvious. How did Bobby feel about being touted as the new Yankee superstar, the successor to Mantle, and the reincarnation of the spirit personified by Ruth, Gehrig and DiMaggio?

It was a poised Murcer who answered them with a self-assurance that belied his 22 years.

"Sure, it's nice to dream about being a superstar," he said. "Any ballplayer would like being one and getting all the things that go with it . . . the television, the opportunities to make some money, and the interesting people you'd meet. But let's face it, even if I'm good enough to be called a superstar some day, I'm not going to do it in one year.

"In fact, I'm not a leader now and I'm certainly not a star. Mickey was the leader here and he's gone. But there are other guys who have been around awhile and have contributed to the success of the club. Heck, just five years ago I was watching all of them on television."

Bobby handled himself so well that he was a popular figure with the media people immediately. But they just wouldn't let go with the superstar bit. Everyone was waiting for the start of the regular season to see if the new Oklahoma kid was the real thing.

They found out in a hurry. The season opened for the Yanks at Washington. In the third inning of that first game, another Bomber rookie cracked a home run over the rightfield fence. Then Murcer stepped in.

Bobby studied the pitcher from his slightly closed stance, midway in the lefthand batters' box. He waggled his bat a few times, then got set. The Washington hurler threw a fastball and Bobby snapped those quick wrists. CRACK! He could feel the good wood from his hands up to his shoulders. And when he looked up, he saw the ball soaring high and deep to rightfield.

He took off toward first, and as he rounded the bag, the ball settled deep in the upper deck. He couldn't believe he had hit it so far. It was a great feeling, and the fans in New York thanked their television sets for allowing them to witness the birth of the next Yankee superstar.

Once again, Bobby had to deal with waves of reporters after the game. It didn't faze him. The next day he went out and belted another one, this time a line shot that rocketed into the lower stands. At the end of the first week, rookie Murcer was batting .393 and the Yanks were heading home. Stadium stalwarts couldn't wait to see their newest hero in person.

And what a debut he made! In the first game he quickly stroked homer number three into the short porch in rightfield. That done, he proceeded to rip a hard double down the line in right. A single to center was his third hit of the afternoon. He had driven home four runs. The youngster from Oklahoma City just couldn't be stopped.

The next day he proved it wasn't a fluke by belting another homer. And the day after that he did it again. Murcer had cracked five homers in the Yanks' first nine games!

Yankee fans wasted no time in discovering Bobby

Murcer. They began to flock to the ballpark as soon as the word was out, and Bobby drew more cheers than any of the veteran players on the team. When someone asked Yankee president Michael Burke if the team was out to create another superstar, Burke answered:

"I don't think you can create a superstar. It's just there in the man himself and all you can do is hope that it comes out. The fact that Bobby's hitting the ball the way he is is just there. We have all seen it together. We don't have to promote anything. The newspapers and television cameras took care of it for us. Now the fans know about it and they want to jump on the bandwagon. They all want to get out and see Bobby now. Then, if he makes it big, they can say they were here when he was just breaking in."

No matter how you looked at it, Bobby was the talk of the town. When the season was just six weeks old, Bobby Murcer was still hitting .324, the fifth best mark in the American League. He had already belted 10 home runs and his runs-batted-in total of 38 was better than anyone else in the major leagues. Everyone was singing the praises of the rookie.

But baseball has always been known as a game of inches. And to some more astute observers, Murcer was beginning to lose the edge. For one thing, he was having a frustrating time of it in the field. Bobby had come to the Yanks as a shortstop in 1965. Now, the Bombers were trying him at third base. It wasn't easy. In those early games which saw him hit the homers and drive in all the runs, Bobby had made 14 errors at the hot corner.

"Bobby was just too erratic with his hands and arm," said Yank manager Ralph Houk. "What it amounted to was that he didn't really know what to do out there."

Then toward the end of May, Bobby injured a heel and missed several games. When he returned, his Midas touch was gone. So was the sweet stroke that terrorized

American League pitchers for six weeks. "I don't know how it happened," Bobby said. "But it seemed that my timing just disappeared."

The rest of the season became a struggle for young Bobby Murcer and the rest of the Yanks. All the high hopes of the spring dissolved into the humidity of the long summer, and the eyes of Stadium fans began to shift out to the borough of Queens, where the other New York team, the Mets, was making some music of its own. Before 1969 ended, all of New York had jumped on the Met bandwagon. The perennial league doormats were en route to an amazing pennant and World Series triumph. Most people forgot there was even a New York Yankee team. And Bobby Murcer, well, he was just a flash in the pan anyway.

How, then, did this well-mannered young man from Oklahoma work his way into the unenviable position of being looked upon as the new Ruth-Gehrig-DiMaggio-Mantle? Blame it on history. It just put him in a certain place at a certain time and told him to produce.

Bobby Ray Murcer was born on May 20, 1946, at St. Anthony Hospital in Oklahoma City, Oklahoma. His parents, Robert and Maybelle Murcer, had two other sons. Dwayne, the eldest, is five years Bobby's senior, while Randy is seven years younger than Bobby.

Unlike the fathers of most top athletes, Bobby's dad wasn't a ballplayer, and he often said of his son: "I'm not sure where he got his ability, but he must have been born with it inside him. He was athletic from the time he was two years old and he always had a ball in his hands from that time on. I used to play catch with him very often and he'd ask me to throw grounders at him, then pop-ups. He loved it, even then."

Bobby's mother describes him as "an ornery kid who ran away from home three or four times when he was young. But he never got very far and used to come back and apologize. I guess he had a bit of a temper even then, but basically, he was a very good boy."

When he reached the age of six or seven, Bobby was playing in the Pee Wee League. He participated in all the sports then, but was already becoming interested in baseball, as were many Oklahoma boys in those days. It was the time when Mickey Mantle was just beginning to make his presence felt with the Yankees, and the boys back home followed their hero's exploits with awe and adulation.

But before long, Bobby was just as active in football and basketball as he was with baseball. They took up all his time.

"So many of the young boys did other things," said Mrs. Murcer, "like play Cowboys and Indians, or fool around with their toy guns. Not Bobby. It was just sports and more sports with him ever since I can remember."

Brooks Moser remembers Bobby, too. Moser was the football and baseball coach at Southeast High School in Oklahoma City. But he met Bobby even before that, when the youngster was one of his students in his eighth grade history class.

"Bobby was a real little guy then," Moser recalls. "He must have weighed all of sixty pounds. I wouldn't have thought that in just two years he would become one of the best all-around athletes I ever coached. But I soon found out that the kid had a heart as big as a watermelon. He was a winner all the way. He thinks win, and that's the most important thing."

The Murcers were also concerned about Bobby's size. After all, he played rough and tumble all day long and most of the other boys were bigger than he was.

"Of course I worried," said Mrs. Murcer. "All mothers do. I didn't think he was big enough, especially for football. But I'll say one thing. Bobby never worried about his size. He didn't let it bother him one bit. And believe it or not, as reckless as he was when he played, he never once got hurt seriously all through high school."

Then Mr. Murcer added, "Sometimes Bobby talked about lifting weights. I really didn't approve of it, except for building up the legs, so he stuck to that. He was aware of being small then, but he always said if Phil Rizzuto could make it as a fast little man, he could too. Even then, he wanted to be the shortstop of the Yankees."

Bobby got tired of baseball once in his life. It happened when he was about 12 or 13. "He just came up to me one night and said he was sick of baseball and he wasn't going to play any more," Mr. Murcer said. "I guess one of the other sports was in season then, because his feeling didn't last long. As soon as it was time again, he grabbed his glove and got back out there."

By the time Bobby reached Southeast High, he was a little bigger, around 5-7, 110 pounds. He never weighed more than 145 at Southwest, so he'll always be remembered as a little guy, even now.

"Pound for pound, Bobby Murcer was the best high school ballplayer I ever coached," said Brooks Moser. "He was tough as a boot, and you can't teach toughness. I remember that he started as a sophomore on the football team and weighed 110 pounds. I knew he had desire and ability, but I wondered about his size. Pretty soon he was challenging guys 40-50 pounds heavier than he was. It didn't bother him a bit.

"Bobby was a running back on offense and a linebacker on defense. By the time he was a senior in 1964, he weighed 145 pounds and he was the hardest running 145-pounder I've ever seen. He was a smart player, too. He always knew what he was doing out there."

On the baseball diamond, Moser was just as impressed with the youngster's skills.

"He started playing for me when he was just a soph,"

the coach recalls. "He had great ability even then. And he had the best batting eye I've ever seen. He was amazing with the bat; he always made contact. In his senior year he struck out just three times and hit about .350.

"He was also a great leader in high school. He always helped the younger boys and gave them his time. Being a star never went to his head. He led by ability and the other boys respected him. He wasn't a power hitter then, but he hit sharp line drives, and got a lot of singles and doubles. He played shortstop for me and did a nice job, although his arm was somewhat erratic."

Bobby was an all-state gridiron and diamond performer for Southeast High, and even found time to make the all-city basketball team. He was a quick guard and averaged close to 20 points a game, though he never loved the court game as much as baseball and football.

In his senior year, he had two outstanding games, one in football, one in baseball, that will always stand out in the mind of Brooks Moser.

"Our football team was playing Harding High for the conference title in 1965. We had a 6-0 lead, and it was late in the game. Harding drove downfield on us and got a first down on the four-yard line. I really didn't think we could hold them.

"On four straight plays, they ran the ball off-tackle. And each time the man who made the initial contact and stopped the play was our middle linebacker, 145-pound Bobby Murcer. He was unbelievable. He must have been really fired up. He just picked the play, filled the hole and stuck the ballcarrier. I always called it a one-man goal-line stand. He really made it possible for us to win that one.

"Then during the baseball season, we had a similar key game against Ulysses S. Grant High, another archrival. All Bobby did that day was get four hits, including a real clout in the sixth inning that he legged out for a home run. And that's the one that won the game for us. It seems he was always coming through in the pinch."

By this time, Bobby was thinking about other things, namely his future. He was a good student with a B-average. Several colleges were already making him scholarship offers because of his athletic ability. But the baseball scouts were coming around, too.

"Baseball was always Bobby's first love," said Brooks Moser. "He always wanted to be a big leaguer. But he really liked the contact and competition in football, too. I think he just realized that baseball offered him a better opportunity for a career.

"Bobby signed a letter of intent to attend Oklahoma University when he was a senior with me. They wanted him as a football player and were thinking of making him a wide receiver. When he asked me what I thought he should do, I told him to go ahead and play baseball if he really wanted to. If he went to college, he might lose his bonus. But if things didn't go well, he could always return to school."

It was a difficult decision that many young men are forced to make. And it's hard to say what the right choice is. Bobby had grown some, but he was still very small for big time football and that might have influenced his decision. Then there was still his old dream.

"Mickey Mantle had been my idol for a long time," he said. "And it was always in the back of my mind to play with the Yankees someday, maybe even on the same team with him. I guess that had something to do with my decision. If the Yankees didn't show an interest, I really don't know what would have happened."

Mrs. Murcer remembers those days well. "Scouts were calling us as early as Bobby's junior year in high school," she said. "I remember the night he graduated, there were five or six scouts waiting by the door. But

Bobby always had his mind set on the Yanks. It was his dream ever since he was a small boy."

Even when the scouts came around, fate was already taking a hand, preparing Bobby for his eventual destiny with the Yanks. The scout who was in charge of the Oklahoma territory for the New York club was Tom Greenwade, the very same man who signed another Oklahoman some 15 years earlier. That youngster's name was Mickey Mantle.

"There's no way I can honestly compare Bobby and Mickey," Tom Greenwade says. "They were different types of ballplayers. Mickey was a switch hitter and Bobby's strictly a lefty. I don't think Bobby ran as well as young Mickey did. And, of course, Mickey was a lot bigger and stronger than Bobby."

Tom Greenwade knows baseball talent as well as anyone. He's been in baseball for some 50 years and with the Yanks for more than 30. Working from his home base in Willard, Missouri, Greenwade roams all over several states looking for young prospects. Though the scouting system has changed somewhat in recent years, there are many similarities from the old days.

"A scout is in charge of a specific territory," explains Greenwade. "And it's up to him to organize that territory. He has to recruit a number of 'bird dogs' or sub scouts who can spot potential talent for him. They can be almost anyone from high school coaches to local businessmen who love sports.

"And the scout himself must be acquainted with coaches and fans. If people know and like you, they'll tip you off to a good kid. And you've got to check every tip, even though sometimes you take one look and know it won't work out.

"These days, scouts generally make regular reports to the parent club. It's necessary under the free agent system so they can be ready to draft. But in the old days, the scout simply knew the openings on the team and worked accordingly. Believe it or not, the Yankees never even knew about Mantle until I had the signed contract with him.

"So it's really up to the scout to make the signing decision. Maybe not with some of the younger guys, but it's always been that way with me. The only time I go to the club for advice is if the boy is asking for too much money, or more than I'm authorized to offer."

Of course, there are specific qualities that scouts look for in young ballplayers and Tom Greenwade has his own particular way of doing it. It's the system he used when he began looking at Bobby Murcer.

"The first thing I look at is a boy's throwing arm," he said. "I worked for Branch Rickey once and he always said that baseball was a throwing game. A boy with a good arm can play somewhere. Then I look for speed. If he can throw and run, that's two of the three qualities. Hitting, naturally, is the third. After that comes the intangibles like temperament and attitude.

"I can tell a 'live' arm very quickly. Then I have to consider the boy's age. Will the arm get better? If a boy can throw and has a good body, then perhaps you can overlook light hitting. Many youngsters chase curveballs and swing at bad pitches. I remember both Pepper Martin and Pee Wee Reese were two guys who couldn't touch a curve when they first came up. But they learned, and before they were through, both were known as good curveball hitters. If, by chance, you find a boy who can hit and pull the ball at the same time, then you've got yourself an exception."

But there's no foolproof method of tabbing a future big league star, and Tom Greenwade doesn't care for the words "can't miss," which are used so often in describing the current season's hot prospects.

"When you sign a kid out of high school, you don't think about whether he'll make it big or not. You simply say to yourself, here's a kid who has a chance. Some make it, some don't. You've got to have reservations because so many things can happen. So much of it depends on a youngster's attitude and determination, plus the tools he has to begin with. I've signed some boys who should have made it, but didn't.

"Then there's the other side of the coin," the old scout continued. "I never realized that Mantle would be so outstanding when I signed him, not until that first season with the Yanks. The same thing happened when I signed George Kell. Then there were boys who I was even higher on and they didn't make it. That's why I never say a kid can't miss."

Tom Greenwade saw Bobby Murcer for the first time in August of 1963. Bobby was playing American Legion ball that summer, waiting for his senior year in high school to begin.

"One of my bird dogs, an insurance man named Howard Parkey, had been watching Bobby for some time. He finally was convinced that Bobby had the makings and asked me to come down and take a look. I told him that we had another scout in the area and I'd get in touch with him.

"Well, this other guy goes down there with Parkey and he's not too high on Bobby. He thought Bobby bailed out against lefthanders and had a bad temper. Parkey contacted the guy again and told him that a lot of other scouts were beginning to look at the kid. But this guy said he wasn't interested. So when Parkey told me about the situation, I jumped on a train and got right on down there. I respected Parkey's judgment.

"I was impressed immediately. Bobby was obviously a good hitter. He made contact and I didn't see any real problems against lefties. He played short and had the good, live arm. But he also had what we call 'hard hands,' but that's something we can overlook at the early stage. If he continued to play the infield, I think he might have overcome it.

"He also had a world of confidence in himself. I liked that. But he did have a bad temper, especially on the football field. I was told, and when I talked to him I advised him to get better control of himself.

"Anyway, I knew that the Red Sox and Dodgers were also interested in him at the time, so I told him not to forget the Yanks and that I wanted to take him to Kansas City for a tryout after he graduated in June."

Bobby then settled into playing all three sports at Southeast during his senior year of 1963-64. Meanwhile, Tom Greenwade was in touch with the Murcer family.

"I think Bobby's dad favored football," he said. "I know Bobby was thinking about baseball then and indicated he was considering sitting out the football season. But his dad wanted him to play and he did. It's lucky he wasn't hurt seriously."

True to his word, Tom Greenwade took Bobby up to Kansas City immediately after he graduated. The Yanks ran a tryout camp there and many of the club officials came down to take a look at the prospects.

Ralph Houk was the Yanks' general manager that year, and he approached Tom Greenwade after the workout.

"What are you going to do about the Murcer kid?" Houk asked.

"I'm gonna sign him," was Greenwade's answer.

Houk smiled. "I hope you do."

After some brief negotiations with Bobby and his family, everything was set. In June of 1964, Bobby Murcer became the property of the New York Yankees. He received a modest bonus, and shunned a rival offer that would have paid him about $1,000 more. He wanted to be a Yankee, though at the time he didn't realize the problems that went along with it. The Yanks immediately assigned the youngster to Johnson City, Tennessee, to play for their farm team in the Appalachian League.

"We were a little worried about Bobby's going so far

away," said Mrs. Murcer. "He had to fly down there and he had never even stepped on a plane before."

But off he went, an 18-year-old shortstop on his way to Johnson City for his first glimpse of life as a professional ballplayer. He had grown since those early days and now stood about 5-10 and was gaining weight. He was almost up to 160 pounds, so he was no longer the little guy. But when he arrived at Johnson City, he found there were some strange things expected of minor leaguers.

"When I got there, I found out that the first thing we had to do was put the field in shape," Bobby said. "In other words, the players were the groundskeepers. We had to pick up rocks and litter, and smooth the whole thing out. I was beginning to wonder if pro ball was everything it was cracked up to be."

But once that was done, Bobby settled down to the business of playing ball. He played in 32 games and was peppering line drives all over the lot. Hitting Appalachian League pitching was no trouble for him. He smacked out 46 safeties in 126 at-bats for a .365 average. He only hit two homers, but he drove in 29 runs. His season was cut short by a knee injury.

"I got banged up sliding into home during the first game of a doubleheader," he recalled. "It's funny, but I didn't even know it at the time. I was sitting out the second game anyway and just relaxed in the dugout. But when the game was over, my knee was twice its size and I could hardly walk on it."

The Yanks didn't want to take any chances with Murcer. They immediately made arrangements for Bobby to come to New York to be examined by the team physician, Dr. Sidney Gaynor.

"I was pretty excited about it," he confessed. "It was my first trip ever to New York, even if it was because of an injury. The only hitch was that my flight landed in Newark, and that really threw me for a loop. I didn't even know how to get to New York from there. Somehow I made it to Dr. Gaynor's office. He found that a sac under my kneecap had burst and there was fluid all over the place. It had to be drained a couple of times, but it wasn't serious.

"The funny part was that I was only in New York for a day. The Yankees were on the road, so I didn't meet any of them. And I didn't even have a chance to go out and see the Stadium. The next thing I knew I was back in Johnson City."

But the Yanks didn't leave Bobby in Johnson City for long. He hit too well for that. The next year they sent him to Greensboro in the Carolina League. That's where he started turning on the power. Playing in 126 games, he had 16 home runs among his 154 hits, and he drove in 90 runs. His batting average was a healthy .322, and the word was that his fielding was getting better. When the Carolina League season ended, the Yanks called him up for the final weeks of the 1965 major league campaign.

Bobby had come in at the tail end of the parade, although he didn't realize it at the time. The New Yorkers had taken their fifth straight pennant in 1964, and their ninth in ten years. Even though they were beaten in the World Series by the Cards that year, it seemed as if the dynasty would continue. There was a blend of old and young players with absolutely no indication that the team was about to decline.

A young ballplayer like Bobby, signed by the Yanks in 1964, could only feel that he was going to the best team in all of baseball and would have a difficult time cracking the starting lineup. How was Bobby or anyone else to know that in the next few years the following things would happen to the team:

Mickey Mantle's great skills would diminish quickly and irreversibly; Roger Maris would be traded; Tom Tresh and Joe Pepitone would fail to live up to superslugger billing; Clete Boyer would be dealt away; Tony

Kubek and Bobby Richardson would both retire prematurely.

No, it was impossible to foresee any of that. But in the 1965 season, the seemingly invincible Yankees suddenly nosedived to a 77-85 record and a sixth-place finish. That's the kind of situation Bobby entered when he was brought up for a "look."

Bobby didn't see too much action with the Yanks. He got into 11 games at shortstop, was unsure of himself in the field, but showed a good batting stroke. He was zero for his first seven at-bats when he came up against righthander Jim Duckworth of Washington.

Duckworth thought he'd fool the youngster with a curve, but Bobby timed it perfectly and sent a screaming liner out toward rightfield. It just kept carrying and finally settled into the lower stands. Bobby couldn't believe it. His first big league hit had been a home run. It seemed all the more unbelievable when one of the players shaking his hand back in the dugout was Mickey Mantle. It was his old dream come true at last.

But that was the only homer he hit. He finished with a .243 average, and four runs batted in. And neither he nor the Yanks had an idea of what awaited the team in 1966. After all, the New York Yankees had been baseball's dominant ballclub since 1920. And when they occasionally fell from the pedestal, they always got up and climbed the mountain again fast.

Not this time. Something wasn't right. The players didn't seem to have the old zip. Then shortstop Tony Kubek was forced into retirement because of a neck injury. Without warning, 19-year-old Bobby Murcer found himself in the running for the starting shortstop position. It was the first of many pressures he was going to feel in the next several seasons.

He started the spring very well. Once again he had the good batting stroke and was meeting the ball solidly. Older players, fans and newsmen said the same thing, "The kid looks like a hitter." He still wasn't sure of himself in the field, but he was getting by, and he figured he'd improve.

Midway through the training season, Yank manager Johnny Keane, who had managed the Cards to a World Series win over the New Yorkers in 1964, told the press that Murcer would get the first crack at the starting shortstop job. In other words, all Bobby had to do was keep things on an even keel and he was the Yankee shortstop.

"Wow," Murcer says now, "that's when I really started to think about it. Maybe before that I didn't realize how close I was to playing major league baseball with the Yankees. I guess I wasn't ready, because when Keane said that I'd likely be the starting shortstop, I was really overawed.

"I suddenly found myself thinking about being alongside all those great players. I really thought the team would bounce back. The thought of my teammates and a pennant race . . . the whole thing overwhelmed me."

And it came out in Bobby's weakest suit—fielding. Suddenly, he couldn't hold onto anything and he couldn't throw straight. The errors came in bunches and manager Keane began to have second thoughts. When Bobby's hitting began to fade, too, Keane made his decision. Veteran journeyman Ruben Amaro would have to play short until Murcer, or someone else, was ready.

"That was a real crusher to me," Bobby said. "I felt like crying when I made all those errors. I knew that I had blown my chance."

So the 1966 season opened with Amaro at short and Murcer on the bench. Amaro played five games for the Yanks. Then there was a collision at second base and the veteran was carried from the field with a severe knee injury. The next day, Bobby Murcer was at shortstop.

The game, played at Baltimore, was a disaster for Bobby. He made three key errors and the Yanks bowed, 5-4. The next day, third baseman Clete Boyer was at short and Bobby was back on the bench. In the following two weeks, Keane used him only as a pinch runner. Then, with the Yankee record at a dismal 4-16, and morale at an all-time low, Keane was fired. And a byproduct of the move that returned Ralph Houk to the field manager's spot, was the demotion of Bobby Murcer to Toledo of the International League. The kid needed more seasoning, they said.

It wasn't easy for Bobby to face another year in the minors, especially in the wake of the great expectations of just a few weeks before. Here he was with the chance of a lifetime, to become the regular shortstop on the New York Yankees. He wasn't yet 20 years old, and Bobby himself blamed his collapse on not being ready, in other words, on immaturity.

Once at Toledo, Bobby settled down. There wasn't the pressure at the minor league club and he relaxed to play his own game. But by midseason, he hit a dry spell and it taught him something.

"Slumps used to really get me," Bobby said. "I'd get down and get depressed. But at Toledo, I learned not to worry about slumps. I was going real good and suddenly I had a spell where I got just three hits in 60 at-bats. After that, I figured I'd never have one as bad as that again. So why worry."

Even with the slump, Bobby finished the 1966 season at Toledo with a .266 batting average. He had 15 homers and 62 RBI's. He showed his usual sharp work with the bat. Fielding was something Bobby still had to work on, and he worried about it. But he looked forward to another good shot with the Yanks in '67.

The reason he knew he'd have a chance was simple. The Bronx Bombers had hit rock bottom. When Bobby came up again at the end of the season, he found a worn-out, disintegrating team. The Yanks were in 10th place, dead last, just two years after taking the American League pennant. Manager Houk used the rookie in about 20 games at the tail end of the year. Bobby batted a disappointing .174 with just 12 hits in 69 at-bats. The team finished with a 70-89 mark and faced a major rebuilding job.

So Bobby returned to Oklahoma, more confident than he had ever been before. Last spring he had been awed by the legendary Yankee stars. Now he'd be trying out for a last-place club. Psychologically, he was in a better frame of mind. He was sure he would make the team in 1967.

That October, Bobby married Kay Rhodes of Oklahoma City, a girl he'd been dating since he was 15 years old. The two of them left for Fort Lauderdale, Florida, the following February. Kay was expecting their first child, and Bobby was confident he'd be with the Yanks for good.

Before he left Oklahoma, Bobby had applied for acceptance into an army reserve unit. He figured there would be little problem and he could work out his schedule as soon as he found which unit he was in. He got a letter, all right, but it wasn't from a reserve unit. It was from the draft board itself. Bobby Murcer had been drafted into the regular Army.

The news was a shock to Bobby, and to the Yanks. Houk and his staff were anxious to take a long look at the kid. Now they'd have to wait two years. It was a bitter disappointment. Bobby and Kay packed again and returned home. He said goodbye and left for basic training at Fort Bliss, Texas.

After Basic, Bobby was assigned to Fort Huachua, Arizona, where he remained for the entire two years. He was with a radio unit and really didn't have to work very hard. But he missed baseball. He hated to lose the two years.

"I really wanted to play some kind of ball while I was there," Bobby said. "But the only way I could play would be to make a 140-mile round trip. And that would be to play a little semi-pro stuff. It just wasn't worth it.

"The only good thing about my army job was that my wife could join me, and our daughter Tori was born right on the army post so I could be close by. I guess that makes her an army brat. She won't believe it when I take her back there some day and show her where she was born."

But time passes, and when Bobby got his release early in 1969, it was almost spring training time again. The Yanks had made some improvement while he was gone. In '67, they were 72-90 and in ninth place. The next year, 1968, the team rebounded to an 83-79 mark and climbed all the way to fifth. But while there were certain plusses that year, there was a major minus, also.

The 1968 season served notice that the end was very near for Mickey Mantle. The one-time superslugger batted a hobbling .237, with 18 homers and 54 RBI's. He was a shell of his former self, struck out too much and played with pain in his battered legs. If Mickey quit, it would signal perhaps the end of another Yankee tradition, the presence of a super ballplayer.

Mantle did quit early in the spring of 1969. And almost immediately, added pressure fell on to the shoulders of young Bobby Murcer.

The first time Bobby took batting practice that spring, he belted clotheslines all over the Fort Lauderdale lot. A close look showed that army life had helped him in one way. He had grown, about 15 pounds worth in the chest and shoulders. He was now 5-11 and a solid 180 pounds. While he could never be considered a Frank Howard or Boog Powell, the days of being the little guy were definitely over.

Manager Houk told the press that Murcer would be given a try at third base. He'd be competing for the job with veteran Bobby Cox, who played there in '69. Cox took one look at Murcer in the batting cage and said,

"I don't know if it will be third or not, but that kid will play somewhere this year. I guarantee it."

Cox was right. Murcer opened the season at third base. And just before the opening game, young Bobby told a reporter about his goals for the 1969 season.

"All I want to do is hit .260 this year," he said. "And I want to stick with the club and help out at third base."

So Bobby was being cautious. Then came the opening day in Washington and his long home run, followed by his sensational start and dramatic home run debut at the Stadium. By that time everyone was looking to him as the next Yankee superstar.

There was even some inside pressure on Bobby. In a completely innocent move, Yankee clubhouseman Pete Sheehy gave him Mickey Mantle's old locker, and also uniform number "1," last worn by Bobby Richardson.

"I gave the kid Mickey's locker because I figured it would make him happy," remarked Sheehy. "I know Mickey likes him and they're both from Oklahoma. Someone might as well use it and why not Murcer?"

Still, it served as another reminder to Bobby of just what was expected of him.

None of this bothered him at the beginning of the season. He continued to hit a ton and drive in baserunners. After two weeks, he ran into a mild slump and went 0-20. This is it, most people thought. The kid will fold now.

But he came out of it April 24, at Cleveland, with a single and two homers. That gave him seven homers in 14 games. He was still hitting .325 and continued to power the ball.

It was the other Yankees who weren't hitting. Both Tresh and Pepitone, expected to take up some of the slack caused by Mantle's retirement, could not get untracked. Neither seemed to want the hat of leadership. Slowly, it was falling on the head of Bobby Murcer.

"Bobby's got the ability and chemistry to make it

big," said Yankee president Michael Burke. "I think he has what it takes to be a superstar. You can't say he's a superstar right now, but he's already a star attraction. And he's a star ballplayer."

All the commotion began to make itself felt. Bobby tried to believe the pressure wouldn't get to him, but he couldn't stop it entirely. In early May, he made four errors at third base in two games as the Yanks dropped their 10th contest in 11 decisions.

The following night against the expansionist Seattle Pilots, Bobby slammed a two-run homer in the first, but Seattle bounced back for seven runs in the bottom of the inning. The Yanks couldn't seem to beat anyone.

Then in the third, Pilot's pitcher Martin Pattin decided to take some action against the Yanks' best hitter. He threw in the general direction of Murcer's head. Bobby was furious. On the next pitch he ripped a single to rightcenter. But he didn't stop at first. He kept running and charged right into Seattle shortstop Ray Oyler.

Oyler couldn't let a young kid push him around and the two began wrestling on the ground. By the time both benches emptied, Bobby realized he was at fault and was apologizing. But it was just another indication of the mounting pressure on the young star.

It was soon after that when Houk moved Bobby to rightfield. He knew the youngster was having a terrible time at third and he didn't want it to affect his hitting. "We considered doing this in spring training," Houk said. "So we were prepared to make the move if we deemed it necessary."

Bobby took it well. Shortly after the move to right, he was the big man at the plate again as the Yanks broke out of another slump. On May 13, he made an error in right, but belted a two-run homer. The Yanks lost that night, their sixth straight, then Bobby got them going again.

He had three singles and a pair of RBI's the next

night and the team won. Then, two days later, the Yanks went into the ninth losing, 1-0, to California. Bobby came up with two out and runners on second and third. Facing lefthander Rudy May, he ripped a double to right and the Yanks won, 2-1.

On May 17, Bobby doubled to open the fourth inning against the Angels and later scored the first run of the game as the Bombers won again. And finally, on the 18th of May, Bobby singled behind Jerry Kenney's single, then Joe Pepitone hit one out and the team won again. Four straight wins, and Bobby was in the midst of them all. A more-than-satisfied Ralph Houk said:

"I'll tell you something, this kid could be one helluva ballplayer. Not just a good ballplayer, but a helluva ballplayer."

Bobby was leading the majors in RBI's with 38 and had 10 homers with a .324 batting average after just six weeks. Then came the injured heel and sudden loss of timing. He began slumping, and this time couldn't seem to snap out of it.

Between May 30, and August 4, Bobby hit just two home runs and his batting average fell some 40 points. During a stretch of games earlier in the season, Bobby had driven in 15 runs while all the other Yankees combined had just 16. Now he was having trouble getting anyone across the plate.

"This kind of thing happens to all young hitters," manager Houk said. "They go good for a while, then they begin to fade. When that happens, they start pressing. But Bobby is too good a hitter not to work his way out of it on his own."

But after several weeks, even Bobby was getting down. "Sometimes I don't know what I have to do to get a hit," he said. "Even when I get good wood on one, someone is there to catch it. But I'm not even hitting the ball that good anymore and I can't understand it. Everything just seemed to go at once.

"At the beginning of the year I hit every ball well

and everything was falling in. Now I think I've been robbed of doubles twice in the last four games. Everything seems to be against me."

But in the end, it was really the pressure that was against Bobby. When he was going good, he'd virtually carried the club. As a 23-year-old rookie who was out of competitive baseball for two years, that pace was just too much to ask for over a long season. Furthermore, the hot start just spiked the talk of a new Yankee superstar, and Bobby heard more than his share of predictions. He was also made to feel that it was his obligation, as the chosen one, to continue the Yankee tradition of having a superslugger on the team.

When it was over, the Yanks had repeated their fifth place finish of 1968, but this time played a whisker under .500 at 80-81. And Bobby finished what would have been a very bright rookie season had it not been for the fast start and aura of great expectations that surrounded him.

He appeared in 152 games, collecting 146 hits in 564 trips to the plate for a .259 batting average. After hitting 10 homers in the first six weeks, Bobby's pace slowed, but he still finished with 26 round trippers and drove 82 runs across the plate. It was certainly a fine freshman season, but with the crosstown Mets winning the pennant, his total performance was all but forgotten by the media and most fans.

Bobby was a popular performer at the Stadium during 1969. He was friendly and courteous to all those with whom he came in contact. He rarely soured, even through the tough months of July and August. But the Yankee rebuilding program was slow. There were no hot prospects in the minor league organization, and other teams in the league were still reluctant to trade with the Bombers. They were all kind of enjoying the mighty Yankees being on the ropes.

The point is this. The Yanks were building a team of singles and doubles hitters. There were no appreciable power men on the horizon. Bubby Murcer was it. Even Tresh and Pepitone had been traded. With his 26 homers and 82 RBI's, he was expected to be the big man, and the pressure on him to take up where Mantle and Company left off was increasing.

Naturally, the men who knew most about the pressure of assuming the role of the big man in the Yankee attack were the two who came before Bobby—Mickey Mantle and Joe DiMaggio.

Someone asked DiMag what kind of pressure there would be on Murcer following the footsteps of himself and Mickey Mantle.

"If he hits .300," Joe D. explained, "there'll be guys who expect him to hit .350. If he hits .350, some people will say he could hit .400.

"Then there will be the boos. Sooner or later they'll boo him. He's just got to learn to accept it. They won't boo him forever. They don't boo anyone forever."

As for Mantle, he left the bite of even more direct comparison, for he and DiMag were both centerfielders.

"If I didn't get to a fly ball, someone would invariably say that Joe would have caught it," Mickey said. "Or if I made a bad throw in a key situation, they'd say DiMag would have cut the runner down. People expected me to do the same things Joe did on the field. When I couldn't do them, the pressure made me try too hard."

For Murcer, the pressure became even greater in 1970 when the Yankees decided he would play in centerfield. "Bobby had the speed and the arm," Houk said. "We knew he was uncomfortable in the infield, although I still believe he would have made it at short or third. He had the tools and he's a plugger. But we wanted him to concentrate on the hitting. We didn't have a centerfielder and we felt it was his best natural position."

Although he knew the comparison with Mantle and DiMaggio would be even more direct, Bobby was happy knowing he had an everyday position. He hoped he could achieve greater consistency than he had the year before.

If Bobby was more consistent in 1970, it certainly wasn't at the high level of proficiency that he had hoped for. In fact, he didn't get his average up above the .250 mark for most of the season. He had to learn a new position again, but he seemed much more comfortable in center than he had been in the infield.

The problem in 1970 was simple. Bobby couldn't get untracked at the plate. He was having some trouble hitting lefties, was striking out too much, and trying to overpower the ball on too many occasions.

"Bobby still hasn't learned that he's a better hitter when he isn't trying to pull the ball so much," commented Tom Greenwade. "And I think the shift to the outfield set him back a bit. Seems like he always had something to slow him down those first couple of years."

The highlight of the 1970 season came for Bobby on Sunday, June 25. The Yanks were playing a doubleheader at the Stadium against the Cleveland Indians. Bobby was hitless when he came up for the last time in game one. He waited for a fastball and pickled it, sending a sharp liner buzzing into the lower rightfield stands for a home run.

Then the first time up in the second game he belted one to almost the exact same spot. Next time up he timed a curve and sent a high, arching drive deep into the seats. It was his third straight homer, and when he came up again, he could feel the tension.

But somehow, he hadn't lost the swing. He picked out a fastball and drove it deep to right. As he dug to first he saw it disappear into the stands for his fourth consecutive homer, tying a major league record of long standing. His teammates congratulated him, but one long time Yankee fan was heard to yell, "Hey, Murcer, why don't you do that more often?"

That was the problem. Bobby just didn't connect enough in 1970. He finished the year with stats very similar to those of his first season, a .251 batting average, 23 home runs, and 78 runs batted in. It wasn't good enough for the partisans still looking for another Mantle.

Surprisingly enough, the Yanks did better than anyone expected. They were never really in the pennant race because the Baltimore Orioles ran away with the American League's Eastern Division. But they played steady ball and finished second with a 93-69 record. Though Bobby had certainly made a contribution, it was overshadowed by the fine play of others.

Leftfielder Roy White was the club's biggest run produced with a .296 batting average, 22 homers and 94 RBI's. He was developing into a consistent, everyday ballplayer. Rookie catcher Thurmon Munson also contributed with a .302 batting average and 53 RBI's. He was also a fine defensive catcher and handled the pitching staff like a veteran, as well as keeping a check on daring baserunners with his strong arm.

The key to the Yankee success in 1970 was the fine pitching. Lefty Fritz Peterson won 20 games, while righties Mel Stottlemyre and Stan Bahnsen won 15 and 14 respectively. In addition, reliever Lindy McDaniel had an outstanding season, with a 9-5 won-lost record, a 2.01 ERA and numerous saves. Some thought the team was coming, but one reporter saw it this way.

"The Yankees are still not a second place team," he wrote. "They lack punch at the plate and need some more steady ballplayers. They had a good season because the pitching held up and because they got some breaks. But the team bears no resemblance whatsoever to the Bronx Bombers of old. There is no team leader and no big man with the bat. The play of young Bobby Murcer was again disappointing, and it's beginning to look as if he'll be a solid ballplayer, but nothing more.

I look for the team to slip back a few notches next year."

Other baseball people agreed with the prognosis. The Yankees had to do some more building before they'd be bona fide contenders. Yet the team seemed content to go with the same people in 1971. They were satisfied with most of the performances. Of Murcer, there was hope that he could get his batting average up perhaps 25-30 points. He was playing well in centerfield and still doing a good job in the power departments. But there was little talk any more of his becoming another Mantle.

Perhaps it was the lessening of the superstar publicity that took some of the pressure off Bobby. For when he returned to Oklahoma City for the offseason, he began to do some serious thinking about the kind of ballplayer he wanted to be in the future.

Bobby took a long look at himself. He stood 5-11 and weighed a solid 180 pounds. He was a tough enough individual, but he certainly wasn't a Mantle, Ruth, Gehrig or DiMaggio. "I'm just not going to hit 40 or 50 home runs," he thought to himself. Then he remembered all the times he went up there swinging for the short rightfield fence and found himself topping a slow grounder to second. In addition, the pitchers were getting cute and giving him very little that he could pull.

"I really wasn't satisfied with my first two years in the majors," Bobby said. "Maybe I wasn't another Mantle or DiMaggio, but I was certainly better than I had shown. And it made me mad.

"Before I even went to training camp, I decided that this had to be a new year for me. Since I knew I wasn't going to be a big home run hitter, I figured I'd better start concentrating on average. I decided to work more on my bunting, and try going with the pitch and forgetting the fences. I struck out more than 100 times in each of my first two years, and I wanted to cut down on that, too.

"I guess it took me awhile to get smart. But I felt things would be better for me in 1971. There are certainly many things that a ballplayer can do offensively besides hitting homers. I knew I had to learn to hit with my head as well as my bat."

When the season began, Bobby stayed with his new philosophy. And there was a marked difference in his batting style. He was hanging the liners all over the place, going to center and left as often as he pulled to right. He started out by jumping over the .300 mark and everyone waited for him to hit his inevitable slump.

But Bobby continued to hit. He was making contact like he did in high school, when you could take a vacation between his strikeouts. There was just one problem. Now that Bobby seemed to be settling into the good groove, the other Yankees were having trouble. Munson was having sophomore jinx problems, Peterson wasn't getting the breaks or the victories, and the bullpen had completely soured. So while Murcer was doing the job, the others weren't and the team was again struggling around the .500 mark.

By midseason, Bobby was still hitting well above .300 and driving in runs. He was chosen the starting centerfielder on the American League all-star team. He responded with one hit in three trips and played a fine game in the outfield. And once again he was being labeled a coming star.

Still, the dull play of the Yanks as a team negated some of Murcer's finer performances. And he began to smart at how his greatest season seemed to be slipping by.

"When the Yanks were always winning and spending each October in the World Series, it was big news whenever someone hit a homer to win a big game. But if I win a game or belt a clutch homer, it doesn't matter because we're still in fourth place."

Yet he certainly wasn't complaining too loudly. "It's

sure a lot more fun coming out to the ballpark every day than it used to be," he said as an afterthought.

Bobby continued his hot pace. In the second game of a doubleheader at Milwaukee on July 25, he came up to pinch hit late in the game. There were three men on base. With a righthander on the mound, Bobby licked his chops. But he wasn't overanxious. He just wanted to make contact.

The Milwaukee pitcher tried to slip a fast one past Murcer. Around came the quick wrists, followed by the sound that always indicated "good wood." The ball soared toward the right centerfield wall and cleared it with room to spare. It was the first grand slam of his career.

When the 1971 season ended, both Bobby Murcer and the Yankees had done complete turnabouts. The Yanks slipped back to fourth place, managing an 82-80 record, the promise of the season before shattered.

As for Bobby, he finally did what they said he'd do two years earlier. With no prolonged slumps or extended dry spells, he put together a super year. His batting average was .331, just six points behind A.L. champ Tony Oliva. He had collected 175 hits (third best in the league) in 529 at bats. Despite not trying for homers, he still managed to wallop 25 and drive in 94 runs. His walks were up to 91 and he cut his strike outs down to a mere 60.

He was also third in the league in total bases (287), had 25 doubles and six triples. And, as one long-time reporter put it, he "enjoyed the best year of any Yankee since Mickey Mantle won the Triple Crown in 1956. And that includes playing the finest defensive centerfield since Mantle was a pup."

Naturally, there was superstar talk again. Was Bobby Murcer finally in that category? The most obvious man to ask was Mantle, and he responded quickly.

"If Bobby can put together two or three years like last year, I'd have to say he could be called a superstar," said Mickey. "He certainly doesn't have to hit 50 home runs to do it. I think Bobby is capable of batting .350."

Yank general manager Lee MacPhail agreed. "Bobby's pretty close to being a superstar right now. It just takes a couple of outstanding seasons for him to establish that fact in people's minds."

Manager Houk also had similar thoughts. "If Bobby has another year as good as this one he'll be recognized as a superstar. He's not going to hit 50 home runs. One thing he has to do is take better advantage of his speed. And, of course, if we can get into a World Series, then he'll get national recognition."

The Yanks had the same basic team in 1972. They added a relief pitcher, Sparky Lyle, and he brought the bullpen back singlehandedly, becoming the outstanding reliever in the majors. His presence snapped the team back into pennant contention.

In the meantime, Murcer watchers wondered if their hero would take up where he left off in '71. Bobby quickly gave them his answer.

No!

The 1972 season started like a nightmare. He couldn't hit. Not a lick. It was just like his rookie year. His timing was gone and he couldn't seem to do anything right. When he did hit a solid shot, it was caught. Suddenly, the young Oklahoman was in a make or break situation. The ultimate direction of his career was at stake right here. Would he be an up-and-down player, with good and bad years, streaks and slumps? He had been striving for consistency since coming to the club. He didn't want to let it all slip away now.

But the players' strike had set training back and that might have hurt. By the end of May, Bobby was batting just .206. He had never been that low before. And the team wasn't winning. It was the year Houk promised to get the Yanks back into contention. Now he was hoping panic wouldn't set in.

It was time for someone to take charge. When it happened, the man turned out to be Bobby Murcer. Suddenly, without warning, he began to hit. He slammed out 15 hits in his next 24 at-bats, including two homers and seven RBI's. By mid-June his average was up to .264, and he was driving in key runs with a mixture of homers and doubles, and whatever else it took.

Bobby was again selected for the all-star team (though not as a starter) and his sensational play right before the midseason game produced this comment from Hall of Famer Ted Williams.

"Bobby Murcer is going to be one of the top stars in the league for the next ten years," the Splendid Splinter said. "In fact, he may just be the best player in the league right now. He's a fine hitter already and he's improving in all the other departments. All he needs now is more experience and confidence. Don't forget, he's only 26."

Even the umpires had respect for Bobby. Ron Luciano talked about a game he called behind the plate. "Murcer sees the ball as well as anyone," Luciano said. "He'll tell you exactly where every pitch is. He missed one strike, but then he told me exactly where the ball was and that really impressed me."

By August, Bobby's slugging and Lyle's bullpen work were instrumental in plunging the Yanks in the midst of a four-team fight for the pennant. It came down to the last weeks of the season, when the team finally fell short. Officially, they were fourth with a 79-76 record, but it was closer than that. The club was still lacking that little extra punch that would put it over the top. But no one could fault Murcer.

Bobby had another great season. Despite his slow start, he recovered to hit over .300 during the second half and finished with a respectable .292 average. In the power department he was devastating, with 33 homers and 96 runs batted in, his personal high in both categories. And he was the big man in the clutch, delivering a bevy of key hits all year.

He also collected 314 total bases, 30 doubles, and seven triples. And he scored a career high of 102 runs. There was little doubt that Bobby Murcer had finally arrived.

"Bobby has become a complete player in the last two years," said Ralph Houk. "He has better bat control now and he takes the walk. He'll go to left and leftcenter and he won't give in to the pitchers. We just hope he continues his current pace."

Before the 1973 season, the Yanks made several trades which they hoped would give the team additional batting power. Once again, the Bombers seemed on the brink of being one of the better teams in the league. There may not be a DiMaggio or a Mantle in the club, but there is a Bobby Murcer. And Bobby Murcer is quickly becoming an outstanding ballplayer and team leader. He himself once said:

"I'm not Mantle and I'm not DiMaggio. I'm Bobby Murcer, and as long as I remmber that, I'll be all right."

Bobby Murcer was telling the truth. He's learned his lesson. He no longer allows the pressure to get to him. The comparisons don't make him try to be something he isn't. He is simply playing the game the way he knows best. And there's no doubt in anyone's mind that it's in the best interest of Yankee tradition.

3. Johnny Bench

If someone asked you to name all the supercatchers in the history of baseball, where would you start? It might depend on your age, or on the amount of baseball literature you've read. Or it might mean parroting some tales told by your grandfather, and then your father before you. But one thing's for certain when you're looking for supercatchers; the list is quite limited.

Pick some names from the early days. Ray Schalk, Gabby Street, Roger Bresnahan. Only a few old timers remember them. Maybe they were great, maybe not. When you get to the middle years of Bill Dickey, Mickey Cochrane and Gabby Hartnett, you usually find the men most widely acclaimed as the best ever.

Later on there were two more great ones, and their names almost always go together. Berra and Campanella. Campanella and Berra. Two great catchers, Hall of Famers, superstars of their era.

A few will say that Josh Gibson was the greatest of them all. But he had the misfortune of being born black into a world that refused to allow his race to play in the majors. So he toiled in the Negro Leagues and never got a chance to show his stuff in the Bigs.

Then there's today. Take a quick glance at the major league rosters and see how many supercatchers you find. Here's one. No, can't throw well enough. Hey, how about this one? No, never hits above .250. What about this one? Oh, he's always hurt, misses 30-40 games a year.

And so it goes. It's hard to find a backstop with all the skills—catching, throwing, hitting, slugging, running—to be classified as an honest-to-goodness superstar catcher. Then you come to Johnny Bench.

Johnny Bench.

Say it again. Johnny Bench. Now you have found your man. For Johnny Bench is surely a superstar, surely a supercatcher. And before he hangs up his spikes for good, some think Johnny Bench will be the greatest of them all.

He's only been in the majors since 1968. But he's done more in that time than most catchers accomplish in an entire career. He's been the Rookie of the Year, the Most Valuable Player twice, the league's homer and RBI champion on two occasions, a two-time World Series performer, and a player representative. He became the instant leader of a veteran team at the age of 21 and has held that position ever since.

As a catcher, he has won the Golden Glove for fielding every year he's been in the National League. And he has one of the strongest throwing arms ever, strong enough to make a Cincinnati pitcher drool: "I wish I could throw the ball like Bench can."

Supercatcher . . . definitely. Bench can do more things well than any backstop of the last decade. As for his own baseball ambitions, Johnny makes no secret of it. On more than one occasion he has said: "There are so many false things in the world today. I never wanted to be a part of them. Sometimes a person who says what he thinks is thought of as cocky or conceited. But if you have a goal in life, you've got to be able to stand up and talk about it. And I want to be the greatest catcher ever to play the game."

Johnny Bench had had his goal for a long time, ever since he was a youngster in Binger, Oklahoma. He was born in nearby Oklahoma City on December 7, 1947. But when he was just a toddler, his parents, Ted and Katie Bench, moved their family of four to Binger, a town John has described as sitting "about two miles beyond Resume Speed."

The Bench family consisted of two older boys, Ted, Jr., and William, then John, and finally a sister, Marilyn. When they came to Binger, the population swelled to near the 730 mark. It's hard to describe a town like Binger to someone who has spent his life in a big city, or even in the so-called country of suburbia.

Listen to John Riggins, the star fullback for the New York Jets of the National Football League. Riggins came from the town of Centralia, Kansas, which was even smaller than Binger. But the two are much alike.

When asked to discuss Centralia for some reporters, Riggins said:

"There's no way you can make it (Centralia) any bigger than it is. I guess you could say we lived 'downtown,' but the prairie started just three blocks away. And there never was much of anything to do back there. When I was a kid, one of the biggest things that ever happened was when my best friend's pig had piglets. We all rushed over to his place and watched. I'll never forget it."

Bench may or may not have seen the birth of piglets in Binger, but he certainly could appreciate Riggins' sentiments. When he viewed a screening of the film, *The Last Picture Show* (a movie set in a one-street town in the southwest), Johnny nodded knowingly at the movie's realism. That's the way it was.

Dave Gunter, a good friend of Johnny's right up through high school, recalls that life in Binger sometimes became rather routine.

"The kids never had anything very special to do in Binger. It was a big deal when someone got the family car and a bunch of us went bowling or to a show over at Anadarko, a nearby town. Some kids got their cars and just drove up and down the main street of Binger, back and forth, all day long."

As for Johnny, he had other interests right from the beginning, namely sports. His father, Ted Bench, was a furniture salesman in Binger, but he had been a semi-pro catcher in his early days and always encouraged his boys to play ball. It wasn't long before young John was playing and competing, usually with his older brothers.

"When Johnny was about five, he was already playing baseball with his brothers," said Mrs. Bench. "And they made it hard for him. They never gave him a break because he was smaller. They made him work for everything.

"A lot of times the boys played 'tin can.' They would

split an old bat down the middle, then get a tin milk can which would be the ball. It didn't go too far and they could play in a small area. I used to hear that can bouncing all over the place around the house.

"But it was always something, either a ball or tin can. And before long Johnny was always swinging a bat or throwing a ball around. He could stand there for hours and just throw a rubber ball up against the house. I don't remember him ever getting tired of playing ball."

Mr. Bench also saw Johnny's early love for the game. He figured his youngest son was going to be the ballplayer in the family and he went to work on him.

"John's dad never pushed him into baseball," recalls Dave Gunter. "He didn't force John to practice or play. No one ever had to force John to play ball. But Mr. Bench created an atmosphere in which John could become a ballplayer. He made sure that John had the equipment and the facilities. He wouldn't let John go wanting for a field to play on or other boys to play with.

"In fact, when John was Little League age, Mr. Bench went out and formed a team right in Binger, mainly so John could get into competition with boys his own age. But when he couldn't get a whole league going in town, he used to drive the boys about 18 miles over to Fort Cobb so they could play in the league there."

By that time baseball was all Johnny Bench wanted to do. He stood up in his second grade class and announced that he wanted to be a ballplayer when he grew up. The other kids laughed. Sure, they snickered, another Mickey Mantle. Mantle, of course, was then in the midst of his great career with the Yanks, and being a native of Oklahoma, all the youngsters followed his feats with wide-eyed idolatry. Mickey was their main man.

When he was reminded of his early self-prophecy, Johnny just smiled. "You know," he said, "I did the same thing in the eighth grade. I got up during a discussion of vocations, and said I wanted to be a ballplayer. And I got the same reaction from the kids. They laughed. But when I did it for a third time in high school, no one was laughing any more."

Dave Gunter moved to Binger in 1959. He met Johnny soon after, and the two played Little League ball together.

"John was a good ballplayer, even then," Gunter says. "He really had the desire. He would rather play ball than anything else and he hustled all the time. But he was all hands and feet then, the biggest hands and feet I ever saw on a kid. As a consequence, he appeared slow. But he was never clumsy.

"Some days, he and I would play ball all day long. We'd start at eight in the morning and keep at it until it got dark. The only time we stopped was to eat, and sometimes we didn't even bother with that."

"You don't have to remind me about Johnny's love of baseball," said Mrs. Bench. "When he wasn't with the other boys he was playing around the house. He always had a ball in his hands and he broke his share of windows with it. Sometimes he wouldn't get home on time for supper, and sometimes he'd sneak out of the house to play ball with Dave and some of the other boys. But he was never bad. I couldn't ask for a better behaved boy."

Then Mrs. Bench talked about another side of her son's life. "Johnny was always exceptional at everything he did. He was always on top. Even though he was playing ball all the time, he got good grades in school. It came natural to him. In fact, he was valedictorian of both his junior high and senior high school classes. He actually started school a year early because of a mixup with his birthday. After about a month, they found the mistake and sent him home. He cried and cried that he wanted to go back, and when the school officials saw how well he was doing, they said it was all right.

"But Johnny was always very mature for his age, even then. He seemed older than the other boys in his class, and I guess he carried that maturity with him right through to today."

By the time John reached Binger High School, he was an outstanding ballplayer and catcher. Ted Bench had seen to that. He was the one who turned John on to catching. His reasoning was simple. There always was and always would be a need for good catchers in the big leagues. Many backstops can catch, but can't hit. The ones who can hit, don't handle the mitt very well. The right combination is always hard to find.

One reason may be that the physical and mental drain on a catcher is probably greater than at any other position. A catcher must "call" the game for his pitcher. He must be aware of the entire game situation at all times, so he can remind and direct his fielders as to their responsibilities.

On each pitch he's got to squat down, putting a constant strain on his legs. Over nine innings, a catcher's legs become almost "dead," losing most of their spring and bounce. And there's always the threat of a split or broken finger from a foul tip, and a serious spike wound from the inevitable collisions at home plate. No wonder most boys shy away from becoming catchers.

There's an old story about the late Rocky Marciano. The Rock, of course, was a great prize fighter and one of only two undefeated heavyweight champions in history. But there was a time in his life when he was thinking of playing major league ball. Naturally, Marciano was a catcher. When he finally decided to forsake baseball and concentrate on boxing, his mother breathed a sigh of relief.

"I didn't raise my son to be a catcher," Mrs. Marciano said thankfully.

But Ted Bench thought differently. He told young John that if he wanted to be a big league ballplayer, he'd have his best chance as a catcher. Since Ted had had semi-pro experience at the position, he was able to give his son some good coaching. The two of them would work on the necessary catching skills for hours on end.

The elder Bench especially wanted John to develop his throwing arm. He taught his son how to grab the ball across the seams to get the maximum speed and straightest possible throw. He also had John practice throwing to specific spots to improve his accuracy. And he had him throw from a catching crouch, not standing up.

"I didn't want Johnny to just be able to throw to second," Ted Bench said. "He had to throw farther. So we practiced throwing up to 250 feet (almost twice the distance from home to second) from a crouch. He really developed well."

But as is the case with most high school stars, John didn't stick to only one position. His coach, Larry Speer, wanted to take advantage of his great talent, so John caught, played some third base and pitched. With an arm like his, they couldn't keep him off the mound.

By that time, John and Dave Gunter were close friends. They both loved baseball and played together all year round.

"We still played whenever we could," Gunter said. "And we played a lot of basketball, too. Coach Speer was great to us. He let us have equipment any time we wanted it and he let us use the school gym if we wanted to play indoors. And when we weren't playing, we used to watch all the games we could on TV. I can even remember John sitting there with a note pad and copying down the interviews that the announcer did with the players after the game. He dug everything about baseball. I guess he still does.

"Anyway, we played together right through high school. John could have played in the minors when he was 15, but he wanted to play American Legion ball over at Anadarko in the summers. The competition was really tops. So we played with the high school in the spring, then the Legion in the summer. That way, we had a pretty full season."

The Binger High team lost just one game in the three years Johnny played. He had a 16-1 pitching record over the last two seasons and batted over .600. Dave Gunter played first, left field and also pitched. At the time, he was also considered a major league prospect and the two boys were almost inseparable.

"Binger High didn't have a football team back then," Gunter recalls. "I guess there just weren't enough boys to make a good program. So basketball was our second sport. In 1965, the team was 30-2, and went all the way to the finals of the state tourney.

"John was quite a ballplayer on the court, too. He averaged somewhere around 28 points a game, made the all-state team and also earned honorable mention on a prep All-America team. He was about at his full height of six feet and must have weighed a good 190 pounds. Naturally, he was a guard. He never liked the game as much as baseball, but he put everything into it and worked to excel."

By 1965, the word on Bench had already leaked out, and scouts from all over the area were coming to the games to see him. His early ambition was to play for the Yankees, since his idol, Mickey Mantle, was still there. But he wanted to play in the majors so badly that it really didn't matter what team he played for.

"I remember just before he signed," Dave Gunter said. "Binger High was playing Fort Cobb and a whole bunch of scouts were there. Well, all these guys were sitting in their cars behind home plate, casually watching the game . . . except when John came up. Then they jumped out with their clipboards and note pads and pressed their noses right up to the screen. After he batted, they went back to their cars again and waited.

"Well, the last time he comes up, out come the

scouts again. And this time he tags one, a long homer to left center. I'll never forget the grin on his face as he trotted around the bases. He was watching those scouts watching him, and grinning from ear to ear."

It was the Cincinnati Reds who were the lucky team. They signed Johnny shortly after he graduated from high school in 1965. The Reds gave him a $10,000 bonus, but as Dave Gunter says, "He would have gone just for the price of a plane ticket."

Although Johnny's lifelong ambition was to play major league ball, the Bench family still had a decision to make. After all, Johnny was just 17. He could have gone to college for a couple of years and still signed, maybe for even more money.

"Johnny considered going to college," Mrs. Bench said. "He was class valedictorian at Binger and a top athlete, so he could have had a number of scholarships. But he wanted to play baseball so badly. We thought he was a bit young to be going right to the minor leagues. But it was his decision and we knew he was mature enough to make it himself.

"When he told us he was going to sign, his father put his arm around Johnny's shoulder and told him if that's what he really wanted, to go ahead. We would both stand behind him."

It's a difficult decision that some young boys have to make, whether to sign or attend college. If a boy signs, then spends five years trying to make the majors and fails, it's even more difficult for him to return to school. But if he goes to school, he still has the opportunity to sign at any time. Only it doesn't always work that way.

"I made the opposite decision from Johnny," said Dave Gunter. "Maybe I didn't have the same confidence that he did. Anyway, I was a year behind John in school, and the Reds drafted me in 1966. My parents wanted me to sign, but I decided to go to school. I went to Southwestern State College in Oklahoma and played ball there while John was already in the minors.

"Then in my senior year I tore a ligament in my arm and that did it. I don't have any regrets, though. I got my degree and I'm coaching now, baseball and basketball at Navajo High in Altus, Oklahoma. There's always the question of what would have happened if I signed, but if the injury occurred in the minors, I wouldn't have had my college education. But I'm happy that things worked out so well for John."

Johnny Bench left a lot of memories in Binger. He was a poised, quick-thinking young man, with fast reactions and a cool head. Plus he's a great competitor, and Dave Gunter had a story to illustrate both qualities.

"I was a junior in 1965 when John left with the class on the annual senior trip. I think they were gone five or six days. And you know how kids are, a lot of horsing around and not much sleep. Well, on the day they got back, we had a Legion game at Anadarko. John and I were on different teams and he got to the ballpark all sleepy-eyed and tired looking. I was pitching that day and figured it would be easy.

"Sure enough, he looked really sluggish, and I struck him out the first two times he was up. After the second strikeout, his eyes narrowed and he looked out at me with the confident grin. 'I'm gonna get you for that, Dave,' he said. And would you believe the next two times up he smacked out a pair of hard doubles. That's the kind of competitor he is."

The second incident isn't as pleasant to look back on. It was a tragedy that could have been a lot worse. But Dave Gunter will never forget how John's quick action may have saved his life.

"Our high school team was coming back from a game at Anadarko in 1965," he recalls. "The bus was rolling down a long hill toward a T-shaped intersection. Suddenly someone in the back hollered that the brakes were gone.

"I remember the second John heard that he grabbed me around the waist and we both dived onto the floor. The bus hit the guard rail, flipped completely over once, then rolled over again two more times. Two of our friends were thrown out of the bus and killed. When the bus stopped, both John and I had our legs hanging out the back door. But he was still holding me around the waist. If he didn't act so fast, I might have been thrown out, too."

Several years later, someone related this story to Bucky Albers, a newspaperman in Cincinnati who regularly covered the Reds. Albers listened, then nodded his head in acknowledgment.

"That doesn't surprise me at all," he said. "Johnny Bench is an unbelievable person. What he did is probably normal for him. He has unbelievably quick reactions."

So Johnny Bench was on his way, boarding an airplane shortly after his graduation from high school and flying down to Tampa to join the Reds' Class A team in the Florida State League.

"It was a strange feeling," Johnny said in later years when he looked back at his first real trek out of Binger. "Here I was, sort of a naive, country boy on a plane heading for Tampa. I remember getting into the airport at about nine o'clock and going straight out to the ballpark. When I got there, the game was going into the ninth inning. They tossed a uniform toward me and told me to dress. The team had no real catcher and I was slated to be the regular. They wanted me in the game right away.

"So there I was, my first night in Tampa, out on the some ball field with guys 24 or 25 years old. A lot of them knew they weren't going anywhere in baseball. After all, if you're 25 years old and still in Class A, things aren't too bright. Some of these guys had a lot of gripes and I had to be careful.

"What I mean is that it was a man's game. It was

no place for a boy of 17. I was doing a man's job and getting a man's salary. I had to act the part or I'd get burned. And ever since that ninth inning back in 1965, I've been a regular catcher doing a man's job."

It must have been quite an experience, and a lesser person couldn't have made the transition so easily. But that ever-present maturity that his mother had spoken about enabled Johnny to fit right into his leadership position. And his physical skills, practiced so diligently over the years, made it possible for him to do a creditable job on the field. But John's sudden elevation to a role of responsibility took its toll, too. And he thinks about it quite often.

"What happened to me is that I missed the years of growing up," he said, "that time from 17 to 21. I just passed right over those years without really living them. A lot of other guys had a whole kind of experience that I never touched, things like college, dances, fraternity parties, dating, the whole bit. They changed gradually. I had to go from being a boy to being a man overnight."

Perhaps there were some other side-effects of Bench's sudden, quick thrust into the big time. "I don't know if it was because of my age or all the things that were beginning to be said about me, but I developed a real fear of failure when I was about 18," Johnny confesses. "I began to wonder if I could live up to all the expectations, my own and those of others."

Johnny lived up to expectations reasonably well as a 17-year-old. Playing in 68 games for Tampa in 1965, the young catcher batted .248, stroking two homers and driving in 35 runs. He didn't set the world on fire, but he didn't embarrass himself, either.

As a catcher, Johnny showed no apparent weaknesses. In fact, Yogi Berra happened to see Bench catch a few games during the year and quickly proclaimed, "He can do it all right now."

But the Reds didn't want to rush him. In 1966, they

sent him to Peninsula of the Carolina League. Johnny played even better in the stiffer competition. He began to develop his power and hit for a higher average. Behind the plate he was superb, as always.

He played just 98 games for Peninsula in 1966, coming to bat 350 times and banging out 103 hits for a .294 average. Twenty-two of his hits went for the distance and he drove in 68 runs. Defensively, he was like a cat, springing out of his crouch to gun down runners like clay pigeons. Some Peninsula fans didn't care whether he hit or not. They just came out to watch him throw.

By midseason, Johnny was the league's biggest draw. He cut a handsome figure, his solid, six-foot, 200-pound frame projecting strength and power. His still boyish face was characterized by high, rounded cheekbones which betrayed his one-eighth Choctaw Indian heritage.

At the plate, he stood midway in the box from the right side, hands down on the end of the bat. His full swing excited the crowds and they were always waiting for him to connect.

His development had been even faster than the Cincinnati club expected. They wanted to get him into even better competition. So after he had played 98 games at Peninsula, he was told to report to Buffalo, the Reds' top minor league club.

Peninsula fans were so sorry to see Johnny leave that they decided to give him a farewell night and told him they were retiring his number permanently. It had to be one of the very few times that tradition was ever practiced in the minor leagues.

John reported to Buffalo and was told immediately that he was the number one catcher. By then, he had expected it. But he quickly ran into trouble. His very first game resulted in a broken right thumb from a foul tip. He was through for the season.

Later that year he had to call on his quick reflexes

again. A drunk driver forced him off the road and John was lucky he wasn't killed. "I got 18 stitches in my head," he recalls, "and my left arm was cut up pretty bad, too. But I was lucky the guy didn't hit me head on."

By 1967, John was all mended and ready to resume his career. This time, the Reds were really watching. They figured their 19-year-old phenom was just about ready. And they were right. In 98 games with Buffalo, Johnny batted .250, but he cracked out 23 homers and drove home another 68 runs. The Reds wanted a closer look and they called him up toward the end of the season.

Shortly after leaving Buffalo, Johnny heard he had been named Minor League Player of the Year. It was the first of many awards he was to win. He was happy, but already concentrating on his new job—major league

He didn't play too much at the tail of the 1967 season, getting into just 26 games. John had just 14 hits in 86 trips with one homer, six RBI's and a .163 average. Yet he had shown his usual poise behind the plate and at the end of the season a Cincinnati club official said, "We expect Johnny Bench to be our number one catcher next season. Barring a complete reversal of form, he'll be an everyday player. We think he's ready."

Johnny was ready, all right. Before the 1968 season ended, he would have put together one of the finest rookie seasons of any player in baseball.

Before the season even started, the word was out on Bench. There was a poll taken of all the National League managers in which they were asked to rate the players, position by position. When the results were in, Johnny Bench had been voted the league's fifth best catcher. And he hadn't yet played 30 major league games!

No wonder the young Oklahoman had a fear of failing. There were so many people with so many expectations. All eyes were on Bench.

Johnny Bench needn't have worried. He came flying out of the gate in 1968. By the second week of the campaign he was performing like a seasoned veteran. He quickly found he could hit major league pitching and hit it with power. His catching impressed everyone. And he took charge.

The season wasn't more than a month old when Bench was directing the Cincinnati defense. He'd move players around in the field and let his pitchers know exactly who was the boss. Pretty soon his teammates were calling him "The Little General." And his veteran pitchers were feeling the sting.

Righthander Jim Maloney was one of the Red mound mainstays. A former 20-game winner, Maloney had respect all over the league as a gutty competitor and rugged individual. But he suddenly met his match in Johnny Bench.

"I'm out there and I've got two strikes on this guy," said Maloney. "I figure I can throw the fastball right by him. Then I see Bench signaling for a curve. I shake him off. He signals for a curve again. I shake my head again.

"Well, here's this kid, still wet behind the ears, and he keeps asking for the curve. So I finally give it to him and don't you know the batter fans the breeze, misses the ball by a foot! I go into the dugout and he doesn't say a word, just sort of smiles at me.

"I never thought it would happen. But here's this 20-year-old kid, actually bawling me out and telling me what to do. He did it all year long. He was like another coach to me. And you know something, I liked it."

Maloney wasn't the only one who took quick notice of Johnny Bench that first year. Before the season ended, veteran baseball men were singing the praises of the kid not yet old enough to vote. (The voting age was still 21 then.)

"He'll be the all-star catcher for the next ten years," said Los Angeles Dodger manager Walter Alston. "On his ability to run a game and protect the plate, he reminds me of Gabby Hartnett." Cubs manager Leo Durocher said virtually the same thing. "Bench handles the mitt like a magician," cooed the Lip. "He's the greatest catcher since Hartnett." And the Giants' Herman Franks called Johnny "the best catcher I've seen in twenty years."

That wasn't all. Former Dodger shortstop great Pee Wee Reese said that John had "the best arm I ever saw hung on a catcher." Some of Bench's teammates agreed. Reds shortstop Woody Woodward talked about his catcher's throws to second.

"You watch the ball coming at you so low and you figure it's going to come in on a hop for sure. But the ball keeps coming. It's never more than two feet off the ground and it kind of explodes on you."

Second baseman Tommy Helms added, "John throws a heavy ball. When you catch it, it stings you."

And perhaps the ultimate compliment that Johnny received as a rookie came from Preston Gomez, who was managing the San Diego Padres that year. Said Gomez: "This is a hard thing for me to admit, but Johnny Bench doesn't have a weakness. Every player since Alexander Cartwright has had a weakness somewhere. Rookies are always loaded with them. But I look and I look and I can't find one with Bench. He's as steady as men who have been around for ten years."

By midseason, Johnny was proving that all the praise was not in vain. He was for real. He was named a reserve catcher on the National League all-star team. And after the all-star game (in which he didn't come to bat) he continued to catch on a day-to-day basis.

His batting style had power written all over it. He stood deep in the box on the right side and held his bat at the very end. He took a long stride and full swing, with a classic follow-through that left him off-balance if he didn't connect. But when he did, the ball left the bat sharply. He hit hard drives to left or left-center. He was a pull hitter all the way, rarely going to right.

But despite his awesome promise as a hitter, it was Johnny Bench's catching that had the baseball world shaking its collective heads in disbelief. Never before in the history of the game had a freshman receiver shown so much poise, so much downright catching and throwing ability.

In a midseason game against the Los Angeles Dodgers, Johnny Bench showed just how much his presence behind the plate could influence a ballgame.

Ron Fairly led off the Dodger sixth inning with a double down the rightfield line. Now catcher Tom Haller was up. The Dodgers needed a run and everyone knew Haller would be trying to bunt Fairly over to third.

Haller was a lefthand batter and Bench called for an outside breaking pitch, one which would be difficult to bunt. The ball broke too much and Haller didn't even go after it. But Bench noticed that Fairly was about four steps toward third. He reached for the outside pitch and gunned his throw to second baseman Tommy Helms. The surprised Fairly slid back to the bag, but the ball was already there. One out.

Then Haller walked. Facing the next batter, the Cincy hurler uncorked a wild pitch. Haller broke for second. John turned to go after the ball. He noticed that it bounded off the boards below the screen. He took three steps toward it, picked it up, whirled and fired to second. Throwing from about 10 or 15 feet behind the plate, he still gunned Haller down with a perfect peg to shortstop Woody Woodward. Two down.

The next Dodger dropped a neat bunt down the first base line. John shed his mask, pounced on the ball and threw the runner out with another perfect peg. Bench's arm had retired the Dodgers single-handedly. It was an amazing performance by a rookie catcher. A newspaperman at the game found it hard to believe.

"I've been a baseball fan for twenty-five years and have been covering the game for ten," the reported said, "and I've never seen a catcher throw like this kid. He gets his throw off in a split second and from any angle. Some catchers wouldn't have even handled the pitch on which he threw out Fairly. He had to lunge for it and was at an awkward angle, but he still got the ball down to second before Fairly could react."

A few weeks later, Johnny gave Cincinnati a big win with a dramatic, eighth-inning homer. After the game, reporters found him sitting casually in front of his locker. One newsman asked him how he stayed so calm in clutch situations.

"I'm not a naturally excitable person," he said, "so I guess I generally look composed. There are some who take that to mean that I don't have nerves. That's not true. I've got nerves just like anyone else. But in an emergency I don't let them take charge. The last thing I'll ever do is panic."

He didn't panic, not once in the 154 games he caught during the 1968 season, and that was a new major league record for games caught by a rookie receiver. His exploits behind the plate that year are already well known. He won the Golden Glove Award as the best catcher in the National League.

As a hitter, John left little to be desired for a 20-year-old with very little prior big league experience. He batted a respectable .275, banging out 155 hits in 564 trips to the plate. He cracked 40 doubles, two triples, 15 home runs, and drove in 82 Redlegs. His all-around effort saw him named the National League's Rookie of the Year by an overwhelming margin, the first catcher in baseball history to win the award. And the Reds moved over the .500 mark with an 83-79 record. The team finished fourth, but was on the rise.

There were more expectations when the 1969 season began. So many rookies fall victim to the notorious "sophomore jinx," which somehow finds them unable to come close to their performances of their initial seasons. Some recover, some don't. The smart money said Bench would take up right where he left off.

"Hell," said one Cincinnati player who was asked about the jinx. "How could Bench be bothered by a sophomore jinx? He already plays like he's been around ten or fifteen years."

The man was right. John came out of the gate like a true all-star, hitting over .300 and driving in runs with his power bat. Behind the mask he was better than ever, running the game and handling his pitchers as if he was their coach of 20 years standing.

"You know you can't throw an inside fastball to that guy," he barked at one of the veterans one day. The pitcher just nodded, followed Bench's advice, and got out of the jam.

Another day, the Dodgers' Maury Wills, a man who once stole 104 bases in a season, took off for a second against Bench. John reached for the ball. It stuck in his mitt. He reached again, grabbed it, and still nipped the speedy Wills at second.

"There's no finer catcher in the league than Bench," said Wills after the game, "and I've seen all the good ones for the past fifteen years. He constantly makes you conscious of his presence back there."

Another time, coaxed by a reporter, Johnny came right out and said, "I can throw out any baserunner alive."

Two days later, Lou Brock took up the challenge. The Cardinal outfielder was the league's current stolen-base king. When he ran against Bench, he had swiped 21 sacks in a row. He didn't make it 22. Bench gunned him down with a low, accurate bullet.

Johnny knew that there would be many challenges facing him in the days, months and years to come. And being a catcher, there were certain responsibilities that the other positions did not carry.

"There are eight other guys on the field," he said, "and each one of them is looking right at the catcher before each pitch. No one looks at the third baseman or the rightfielder. I've got to be able to give the pitcher confidence, the confidence that I'm calling for the right pitch. If I motion to a fielder to move up or back a few feet, he's got to know that I'm aware of the game situation, the hitter and the pitch or sequence of pitches I'm about to call. He's got to believe that I know what I'm doing.

"I think part of all this is being confident. I know people say you're supposed to duck your head and look humble when someone praises you. But why should I? I've got a lot of people depending on me and I know what I can do."

A perfect example of the fine detail that must be filled in a catcher's mind came in a late-season game at Houston during the 1969 season. Cincy led the Astros, 2-1, in the bottom of the ninth. Relief pitcher Wayne Granger was in the game and facing pinch hitter Keith Lampard, a rookie. There was a runner on first.

The word on Lampard was to pitch him inside. Johnny called for an inside fastball and it nipped the corner for a strike. He was going to go to Granger's best pitch, the sinker, but changed his mind and called for the inside fastball again. This time the lefthand-batting Lampard swung and drove the ball deep into the right centerfield stands for a game-winning homer.

Afterward, Bench explained what had happened. "It was the right call," he said. "And with any other pitcher it would have worked. But Wayne's a sidearm pitcher and his fastball tails out a few inches. That made the difference. And I forgot about it. You've got to remember that all your pitchers are different. One guy's fastball or curve might work against a particular hitter, while the other guy's won't."

But that was one of the few mistakes Johnny Bench made. By midseason he was hitting well over .300 and with power. He was named the starting catcher in that year's all-star game and responded with a homer, single, walk and two RBI's. The 21-year-old Bench was showing that he could cut it with the best of them.

One of the reasons for John's success was his physical assets. A compact six-footer, weighing about 205 pounds, Bench packed power and plenty of it into his shoulders, arms and legs.

"His type of build is pretty scarce in baseball these days," said Reds' trainer Bill Cooper. "Those kinds of guys usually play football. I don't think there's a guy on this team who could pin Johnny in arm wrestling. And his hands are so big that he can hold six baseballs at the same time in either one of them."

The Reds were in the pennant race in 1969, making a strong bid until faltering late in the season. They finished third with an 89-73 mark and had the makings of a winner. Bench had joined with power hitters Tony Perez and Lee May to form a trio of potent RBI men. Pete Rose and Bobby Tolan provided speed and hustle. With a little more pitching, the experts figured the Redlegs might put it all together in 1970.

As for Bench, he lived up to preseason predictions and totally defied any kind of sophomore jinx. A late-season slump dropped him below .300, but he still wound up at the .293 mark. In addition, he pounded out 26 homers and drove in 90 runs. He seemed to be developing right on schedule.

But if there was a schedule, Johnny must have skipped a couple of steps in 1970. With a new manager in Sparky Anderson, and improved pitching with American League castoff Jim Merritt, and rookie Wayne Simpson, the Reds began to move early. And the prime mover in the power attack that became known as the "Big Red Machine" was Johnny Bench.

Batting cleanup and hitting with more confidence than ever before, Bench tore apart National League pitching. By midseason, he had burst to the top of the majors in both home runs and RBI's. The Redlegs fulfilled their promise and were way atop the National League's Western Division. It looked like a runaway.

By early September, Cincinnati had wrapped up the pennant. The big Red bats treated everyone the same, rudely and roughly. When it wasn't Perez, it was May. When it wasn't May, it was Rose; when not Rose, then Tolan. And when they failed, Bernie Carbo, Hal MacRae, Tommy Helms or Woody Woodward picked up the slack. But through it all, the main man was Johnny Bench.

When the season ended, Bench's stats were imposing. The young catcher led the major leagues with 45 home runs and 148 RBI's. Plus he batted .293 for the second year in a row. He had 177 hits in 605 at-bats, and had played in 158 games. In fact, when manager Anderson felt that catching every day was getting to his star, he played Johnny at other positions, usually third or the outfield. Wherever he played, John did the job well.

Some people thought that the moves were a foreshadowing. With John hitting so well, who knows how good he'd be without the burden of everyday catching to contend with? But Johnny quickly put an end to those rumors. He told newsman Bucky Albers about his reasons for wanting to remain behind the plate.

"Johnny's no fool," said Albers. "He knows the score. He's one smart kid and he was from the time he came up to the Reds. I remember his high school coach, Larry Speer, once telling me that he thought John could out-think any two people thinking at the same time. That's the way he phrased it.

"Anyway, the point I'm making is that John knows he's an all-star backstop. He's aware of the fact that he's got exceptional ability as a catcher. He once told me that playing any other position he's just another ballplayer, at least in the field. So he's not about to stop doing what he does best and what he's trained to do for so long.

"I remember one day when he played the outfield and Pat Corrales caught. It was a real hot day and after the game John kidded Corrales about how full of dirt and sweaty he was. Then he pointed to himself, all clean and relaxed, and he laughed about it. But later he admitted that he tends to let his mind wander in the outfield and almost feels like going to sleep. He misses the excitement and responsibility of catching."

As for his catching, Johnny Bench was already the undisputed best in the game. He did everything well, and he was getting better. To begin with, it's said that Bench gets down lower than any catcher in baseball. He keeps his glove some four to six inches lower than the others and as a result gives the pitcher a better target.

He's also very aware of the difficulties catchers have with low balls. He had some himself his first couple of years in the league. Now he's so fussy that he carefully smooths out the spike marks around the plate after each hitter has come up. He doesn't want any bad bounces when he's back there. The system seems to be working. Bench was charged with 18 passed balls as a rookie, and 14 in his second year. But he had just three in the first 100 games of 1970 and kept that ratio throughout the season.

Johnny also rarely catches warmup. And if he does, he always wears all his gear. "Some catchers warm up the pitcher without their equipment," John explained. "So when there's a pitch in the dirt they duck out of the way and swipe at it. That breeds bad habits. If you're going to warm up a pitcher, you've got to catch exactly as you would in a real game."

Early in his career, Johnny converted to the new one-handed style of catching. The traditional two-handed way had the receiver using both hands to grab a pitch. That resulted in many hand and finger injuries. And catchers were always worried about being hit by a stray foul tip.

The one-handed style utilizes a larger, hinged mitt, something like a first baseman's glove. The catcher snares everything in the big mitt with one hand and protects his exposed hand by shielding it behind the glove or outside the right knee.

John practiced the new style for hours, especially sweeping the ball from the mitt to his bare hand for the throw. He had to make a clean exchange and at the same time be sure he gripped the ball across the seams. Once he mastered that, he picked up right where he left off as the best thrower in the game.

"I like to throw from the top and come down with the ball," he explained, "something like pulling a window shade. The throw to first is the quickest release, and is snapped off with more wrist and less arm motion. It's more of a pick-off throw.

"When you throw to second or third, you're usually trying to catch a runner stealing, so you've got a little more time to throw with your arm and body before releasing the ball."

Bench's effectiveness against the steal can be measured once more with statistics. Base runners are usually successful on 70 percent of all steal attempts, and the top men do much better than that. John likes to keep them under 50 per cent, and he's generally been successful.

For the first 100 games of the 1970 season, the top four basestealers in the League (not including the Cincy speedsters), had swiped 113 sacks. But amazingly enough, only one of those steals came against the arm of Johnny Bench. That shows just how much respect they have for the Bench cannon.

After the 1970 season ended, everyone was singing

the praises of Johnny Bench and the Big Red Machine. They made it look easy in the divisional playoffs against the Pittsburgh Pirates, taking three straight games to enter the World Series. Cincy would be meeting the American League champion Baltimore Orioles. Most experts figured it to be a hitters' series. The Reds' pitching staff was crippled by injury. Baltimore had the arms, but who could stop those Big Red bats?

Game one in Cincinnati saw the Reds' Gary Nolan pitching against Jim Palmer of Baltimore. With one out in the Reds' first, Bobby Tolan stroked a double to right. After Tony Perez went out, Johnny Bench came up for his first at bat in world series competition.

More than 50,000 fans at brand-new Riverfront Stadium were on their feet and cheering. It was music to Johnny's ears. Palmer tried a fastball and Bench stepped right into it, sending a liner to center for a base hit. The speedy Tolan streaked home with the first run and Johnny Bench had his first series hit and initial RBI. A two-run homer by Lee May made it 3-0 in the third. It looked as if the Big Red Machine was already rolling.

But then the tide changed. A two-run homer by Boog Powell, and solo shots by Ellie Hendricks and Brooks Robinson gave the Birds a 4-3 victory. Palmer, with relief help from Pete Richert, had shut off the Cincy bats after the third. Johnny didn't get another hit, and a disputed call at home plate, plus a tremendous backhand stop by Brooks Robinson at third settled the issue.

The game set the pattern for the series, especially for the role that the great Brooks Robinson was going to play. In the second game, Cincy opened it again, getting three unearned runs in the first, and another tally on a Tolan homer in the third. But the Birds got one back in the fourth. Then came the Oriole fifth.

All of a sudden it looked like the Big Baltimore Machine. Chico Salmon, Don Buford and Paul Blair whacked out base hits for one run. Starter Jim Mc-

Glothlin was removed and Milt Wilcox took the mound. He was greeted by singles off the bats of Powell and Brooks, followed by a double by Hendricks. When relief ace Clay Carroll came on, the Birds already had five runs and a 6-4 lead.

It was still 6-4 when Johnny came up in the sixth to face veteran righthander Moe Drabowsky. Drabowsky tried an off-speed pitch, but Johnny timed it just right and let loose, smashing a long drive over the leftfield wall. He felt good circling the bases to a standing ovation, but his team was still behind by a run, 6-5, and that's the way it ended. The Birds had a 2-0 lead and the series was moving to Baltimore.

This time it wasn't even close. Baltimore exploded for a 9-3 win, with two doubles by Brooks Robinson and a grand slam homer by pitcher Dave McNally the telling blows. Cincy was trailing, three games to none, and it looked pretty black.

A three-run homer by Lee May gave the Reds a reprieve in game four, 6-5 but in the fifth game, the Orioles erupted again. This time they spotted Cincinnati a 3-0 lead. Then they proceeded to score two runs in each of the first three innings and go on to take the final game, 9-3, and the series, four games to one.

It was a disappointing series for Johnny as well as the other Redlegs. He knew he was expected to hit well, but he managed just four hits in 19 trips for a .211 average. He had one homer and just three runs batted in. Although he was robbed of at least two or three more hits by series MVP Brooks Robinson, it didn't take away the hurt.

But Johnny knew how to bounce back from a loss. Several weeks later he was greeted by the news that he had been named the Most Valuable Player in the National League. And once the handsome catcher hit the papers as the MVP, everyone wanted him. He was suddenly one of the most sought-after celebrities in the country.

He was invited to banquets, had offers to do commercials and appear on TV shows, and finally he was offered a show of his own. Plus he appeared as an entertainer in Las Vegas, and toured Viet Nam with the Bob Hope Christmas Troupe. And he was loving every minute of it.

"John has always been fascinated by show business," said newsman Bucky Albers. "He likes the show biz people and they like him. I was always struck by the unbelievable amount of poise that he has. I remember when he got his TV show and went to San Francisco to tape the first one. It was a talk show, with celebrity guests. Well, he didn't have any TV experience, and you'd think he'd be nervous as a cat. But they handed him the microphone and when the red light went on he said, 'Hello, I'm Johnny Bench,' and he took it from there. He was so cool I couldn't believe it."

But just when it looked as if things couldn't be better, John had to face the biggest crisis of his young life. He came into the 1971 season hoping to have another good year and help lead his club back into the World Series. Despite a busy winter of activities, including a turn on the famed banquet circuit, he seemed fit and ready to go.

And when he hit nine home runs and batted .312 in the month of April alone, it looked like he was on his way. The so-called experts said he'd go over 50 homers this time for sure. But it was Johnny himself who later cast the first shred of doubt on the season.

"I remember we were playing the Giants on the night of April 30," he recalled. "Juan Marichal was pitching and I hit two home runs off him. But we lost the game. I just had a funny feeling that night that it wasn't going to be like 1970 this time."

There was one basic difference already. Bobby Tolan, the Reds' swift centerfielder, was out for the year with a ruptured Achilles' tendon. So the team lost its top baserunner and sparkplug. Plus the pitching was again questionable. John felt even more pressure to produce.

The season moved into May and the Reds were still playing below .500 ball. On the 17th of the month, John stepped into a Jim Bunning fastball and sent a high homer over the leftfield wall. The public address announcer informed the crowd that it was the 100th homer of Bench's short career. It was also his 13th of the season. But by the end of May his average was well below .300 and his power production was slowly ebbing. And suddenly the question was being asked: What's wrong with Bench?

By all-star time in July, John was struggling around the .250 mark. Other Cincy stalwarts were also having sub-par years and it was beginning to look as if the team wouldn't repeat as N.L. champs. But when the votes were counted, Johnny Bench was again the starting catcher on the National League all-star team.

Johnny had a sore wrist and bruised hand the week before the game. For a while he was a doubtful starter. He didn't touch a bat for the six days directly preceding the game. But when the starting lineups were announced at Detroit's Tiger Stadium, Johnny Bench was there.

"The game was very important to me," he said later. "Vida Blue was scheduled to start for the American League. He had a 17-3 record in just half a season and they were calling him the fastest pitcher since Sandy Koufax. I wanted to see for myself."

In the second inning, Willie Stargell was hit by a pitched ball, and Bench stepped up. Blue unleashed a blazer and John fouled it off. He knew that Blue would challenge him again and he dug in, waving his bat out toward the mound and expecting to see the lefthander's fastball for a second time.

He was right. Blue tried to blow it by him, but John

was ready. He stepped into the pitch and felt that good vibration in his wrists. The ball left the bat faster than it came in and streaked out to left center. It never stopped climbing until it settled into the upper tier for a home run. Bench had met the challenge of Blue and had come out on top.

Later in the same game, John rapped a single and hit the ball hard two other times. It was difficult to believe he was struggling, but as soon as he returned to regular competition, the woes returned.

Soon it became obvious that Bench wasn't coming out of the slump. By August, he was hearing a new sound, one that he'd never heard before in his life. That sound was booing. The frustrated Cincinnati fans began to take out their anguish on John.

When the season ended, the Giants had won the N.L. West, while the Redlegs finished fourth with a 79-83 record, a far cry from the pennant-winning 102-60 mark of the year before. Johnny's personal totals were appalling. He finished the year with a .238 batting average, 27 home runs, and just 61 RBI's.

It wasn't the Bench people had come to know. Right away everyone had an opinion as to what went wrong. Most of it led to the same thing. John's popularity boom of the year before had gotten to him. He was involved in so many other things that baseball was no longer number one. He wasn't concentrating.

One veteran coach put it this way. "Coming out to the ballpark was no longer the single most important thing in his (Bench's) life." While a major league manager diagnosed the problem by saying, "It's too bad. First the Most Valuable Player Award, then the television and the glamour . . . all that stuff can take a young man's mind away from business."

Redleg coach Ted Kluszewski, a former slugging star himself, thought the problem was simpler and related strictly to the nuances of the game of baseball. "John got into a bad habit," big Klu said. "He was trying to sweep everything out of the ballpark instead of just meeting the ball with that good, compact, short stroke like he had last year. He's gonna hit some home runs when the ball's in the right spot, but he won't hit consistently with a swing like that."

Of course, the man to really ask about Johnny Bench's 1971 season was Johnny Bench. And John explained how the middle just dropped out on him.

"I started out pretty well, especially for me because I've never been a really fast starter. Then there were the two homers against Marichal when we lost, 5-4. We were supposed to be the good team and they were beating us. We just weren't putting it together.

"Then in the early summer I had to go to summer camp as part of my reserve duty. My two-week routine was to get up at 4:30 in the morning, drive two hours to the base, do my army duty, then drive back to Cincinnati, play the game, catch a couple of hours sleep, and start all over again at 4:30 the next morning.

"After two weeks of that the team started on a road trip, then I hurt my wrist, and it was almost two months before I settled into a comfortable routine again."

Newsman Bucky Albers was another witness to Bench's struggle in 1971. "I think John started by trying to hit everything out of the park," Albers recalls, "and for a while he did. But then he began tailing off. When that happened, he started to press. Then the fans got on him and he tried harder. It was just a step-by-step progression. And when it finally got so bad, with the team out of it and everything, he got down and stopped trying.

"I think he sort of lost control of the strike zone by the end of the year. It was probably a result of everything else that happened."

Reds manager Sparky Anderson agreed with Albers' last statement. "John must learn to contain himself at the plate again. All year long he was lunging at pitches out of the strike zone. He's had a terrible time of it but he's too much of a natural to let it happen again."

Then John let it be known that he was going to spend two weeks with the Cincy rookies in the Florida Instructional League. "I swing the bat as hard as anyone," John said, "and with my weight and the right swing, I should be able to hit home runs. But I've got to learn the strike zone better and that's why I'm going to Florida."

So he went south after the 1971 season ended. There was Johnny Bench, superstar, cavorting with raw rookies of 18 and 19, and enjoying himself. Bench is never too good to hang out with anyone. And when the two weeks ended, he said he felt better about his swing. He then rushed off to resume his busy winter schedule.

It was that schedule that had some of the Cincy brass worried. Was the youngster continuing to extend himself too much? Some thought it better if he concentrated on baseball and nothing else, especially in view of the year just past.

"I really don't think my outside activities hurt me too much," John said when questioned. "The TV show was usually done on an off-day and it was fun. Plus it's an investment for my future. I'll have it again if they want me. Some of the management people at Cincinnati thought I should have less administrative responsibilities in some of my outside interests. I've taken care of that. I'm ready to play ball again right now."

One thing that bothered John greatly was the boos. The fans' reaction to his off-season was difficult for him to understand. As Bucky Albers said, "John accepted failure like a man, though he didn't like it. He lived with it. He showed his class. But he did tell a writer in Florida that he wasn't going to tip his cap to the fans in '72. He was still thinking about those boo birds. But once the season started, he forgot about that, too."

The season started on a high note for the Reds. A

big trade with Houston saw them lose slugger Lee May, but gain Joe Morgan, a fiery second baseman with a world of speed. Tolan seemed recovered from his Achilles' tendon injury, and it looked as if the team would have more speed than ever before. John, Tony Perez and newcomer Denis Menke would provide the power.

Johnny looked forward to the new season and to redeeming himself. But all of a sudden it was 1971 again. Maybe he was too anxious, maybe something else, but big John produced just one hit, a weak single, in his first 22 at bats. The boo birds took up right where they left off, with Bench as their favorite target.

And more knowledgeable baseball people wondered if John had a weakness that was finally discovered by the National League pitchers.

But slowly, ever so slowly, Johnny showed signs of working out of it. By the end of May he had his average "up" to .246. The Reds were in third place, four and one-half games from the top. But Tolan, Morgan and Rose were all doing their jobs, hitting and running. Now the power men had to produce.

Shortly afterward, in Houston, John hit a long, deep drive to left center. It caromed off the wall and away from the converging Houston outfielders. John put his head down and ran. By the time the ball came back to the infield, Bench was steaming across home plate with the first inside-the-park homer of his career. And it was a sign of better things to come.

Later in the same game, John smacked a bases-loaded single, then rapped a solo homer to give the Reds the win. The next night he homered again, his ninth of the year, and later commented, "I haven't felt this good in two years."

Cincy fans and Johnny's teammates held their breaths. It was the old Bench, all right . . . but would it last?

He had a key single in a big, 10-3, win over Houston

the next night and the team moved on to Philadelphia.

The Phils were leading the first game, 1-0, in the seventh. John came up and promptly blasted a long homer over the centerfield fence, tying the score.

The game was still tied when John came up with two on in the 17th inning. You guessed it. He walloped another long homer and the Redlegs had another victory. The next night it was more of the same, two home runs. Then someone opened the record book. Sure enough, John's seven homers in five games tied a record set by Jim Bottomley of the Cards way back in 1929.

And he wasn't through yet. He beat the Phils the next night with a two-run double, then moved on to Montreal where he promptly went four for six with three more RBI's. When the Redlegs returned home, John had collected 21 hits in his last 51 at bats, with nine homers and 24 RBI's. His average was up to .306, and he had returned to the top of the league in homers and RBI's.

Johnny Bench was back where he belonged, and so were the Reds, in first place for the first time since 1970. And when John smacked his 16th homer of the year several days later, he tipped his cap to the packed house at Riverfront Stadium. Now everything was back to normal.

For the remainder of the season, the Big Red Machine rolled, easily regaining the National League's Western Division pennant. And John was right back on top, leading the majors in homers with 40 and runs batted in with 125. His batting average dipped slightly in the final weeks but was a respectable .270.

The stats weren't quite up to 1970 standards, but as Bench himself said, "That (1970) was a super year. I know people expect it of me, but I may never come up to that again."

It didn't matter. He was pretty close. Now the Reds had to battle the powerful Pittsburgh Pirates for the right to enter the World Series.

The playoff round was hard fought from the first. The Pirates led, two games to one, and seemed on the brink of wrapping it up. In fact, they had a 3-2 lead in the ninth inning of game four and their relief ace, Dave Guisti, on the mound.

With one out and no one on, John stepped up. He knew that the whole season was riding on this inning. He bit his lip and tightened his grip on the bat. There were two strikes on him and Guisti had the advantage. The Pirate Pitcher threw a fastball on the outside. John took the big swing and hit a rising liner toward right-center. It kept climbing. Al Oliver and Roberto Clemente converged on the ball, but it was out for a home run. John had tied the game.

The Reds then pushed across another run in the same inning, winning the game, 4-3. The next day they took it all with another victory.

"It was really amazing," said Bucky Albers, who was covering the game. "Guisti had two strikes on him but John wasn't just protecting the plate, he was still going for downtown. He fouled one off, then connected with an outside fastball. It was one of the few opposite-field homers I've ever seen him hit. He really has tremendous strength. He wasn't going to give in."

John's second World Series in three years proved to be just as disappointing as the first. The Reds were facing the Oakland Athletics, and were favored to win. But in the first game, Oakland got two homers from a virtually unknown catcher named Gene Tenace and won the game, 3-2.

In game two, also played at Cincinnati, Oakland took a 2-0 lead and held it into the ninth. Then Tony Perez singled and Denis Menke hit a drive to deep left. It looked like it might tie it . . . that is, until Oakland leftfielder Joe Rudi made a leaping, twisting catch up against the wall. It broke the back of the rally and Oakland had another win, 2-1.

Johnny had three hits in the first two games, as did

fellow slugger Tony Perez. But it was the Reds' pepper-pots, Rose, Morgan and Tolan, who were being shut off. Cincy just couldn't put it together.

With the series moved to Oakland, Cincinnati got some surprise pitching from veteran Jack Billingham to take a 1-0 victory and get back in it. But it just wasn't the kind of series the Redlegs expected. Oakland won again to take a 3-1 lead, then Cincy bounced back to make it 3-2.

In the sixth game, John started it off against his old friend Vida Blue by blasting a solo homer in the fourth inning. Before they finished, the Reds had exploded for an 8-1 victory and had tied the series at three games each. Now, with one crucial game remaining, they had a chance.

But it was the A's who were playing under the lucky star this time. The game was tied, 1-1, going into the Oakland sixth. Then doubles by Tenace and Sal Bando got two more runs home and Oakland hung on to win it, 3-2, and take the series, four games to three.

The series MVP was the little-known Tenace, who tied a record with four homers and drove in nine runs. The other catcher, Johnny Bench, was just six for 23 with one homer and one RBI.

Several weeks after the series ended, it was announced that Johnny Bench had been chosen the National League's Most Valuable Player for the second time in three years. He was only the sixth player in National League history to win the award more than once.

It was a satisfying moment for John, because it signalled the completion of his comeback year. Even the loss in the World Series didn't mask his happiness at being named MVP.

"This makes me very, very happy," he said. "I didn't know if I'd get it or not. But it's been very sweet to be able to come back, especially after some of the things I heard about myself last season."

So it seemed that Bench was all ready to resume his role as the top young player in the game. But then, near the end of November of 1972, came another announcement from Cincinnati that shocked the sporting world.

It was revealed that a pre-playoff physical examination showed the existence of a spot on Johnny Bench's right lung. Doctors did not deem it an emergency at the time and John was allowed to compete in post-season games. But if further tests failed to reveal the nature of the spot, surgery might be necessary.

People all over the country began watching for reports from Cincinnati. No one wanted to think the worst. After all, John was just about to celebrate his 25th birthday. Finally it was announced that the spot, or lesion, as it was now called, would have to be removed. John's personal physician, Dr. Luis Gonzales, said he believed the lesion to be benign. He would perform the surgery.

"I'm going to be 100 per cent," John said, acting cheerful before the operation. "That's what the doctors say and that's what I have to believe. I have to think of it in that manner."

The operation took place in mid-December. When the announcement came, it was welcome news. The lesion was benign (non-cancerous) and had been caused by a fungus infection. John was expected to make a speedy, complete recovery and be ready to start the 1973 baseball season.

By Christmas, John was home with his parents, looking a bit thin, but cheerful. He had already received some 15,000 letters from well-wishers all over the country, ranging from kids barely old enough to write, to veteran baseball fans from another era.

"I've gotten an awful lot of letters from young kids," John said. "Most of them were really sympathetic. A lot of them wanted me to get well so I could hit home runs."

Johnny Bench is a man of his time. In his first post-surgical photo, he was trimming a Christmas tree and was wearing a T-shirt with Mickey Mouse embroidered on the front. Yet he is loved and respected by young and old alike.

"John's always been a great sport and natural showman," says Bucky Albers. "The Reds were in Atlanta last year for a doubleheader. Between games there was a special game between the Braves' players and their wives. Now, in Atlanta there's a girl they call Suzy Sweeper. She comes out and sweeps the bases and home plate in the middle of the game. For the husband-wife game, they asked John to be Suzy Sweeper.

"First of all, when would you ask a visiting player to do something like that? He's waiting for the game to start so he can beat you. But Johnny Bench is different. When it came time for Suzy, out ran John in his baseball cap, usual number "5" jersey, spikes . . . and white shorts. He swept all the bases while the fans howled and applauded. Then he went over to the guest umpire, heavyweight boxer Jerry Quarry, and kissed him on the cheek. That wasn't in the script, but John ad-libbed it. He's a natural showman and he loves to entertain people."

But Johnny Bench is also deadly serious about his baseball. When he was just a rookie, Ted Williams autographed a ball for him. On it, Williams wrote: "To Johnny Bench, a Hall of Famer for sure." Well, Johnny Bench doesn't want to led Ted Williams down . . . or anyone else for that matter.

His MVP year of 1972 got him into the $100,000 class in salary and there are few who will say he doesn't deserve it. He's already given Cincinnati fans more than their share of excitement.

Johnny lives in a seven-room condominium in a fashionable section of Cincinnati. He enjoys his life as a celebrity and a bachelor, often dating beautiful show business girls. But he doesn't restrict himself to any one type of person. He also enjoys cooking and listening to music. He's very conscious of the lyrics of many of today's songs and has taken a turn or two at singing them himself. He says he wants to get married and have children someday.

Despite a full schedule, he's never too busy to visit a local hospital and talk to the kids there. He'll often do this on the spur of the moment, during an off-day or in the morning before a night game.

Johnny Bench once said that he missed three years of his life. Now he can enjoy some of the things that were missing when he was working his way to the big leagues. But he's still careful and selective about what he does. As usual, Johnny Bench thinks everything through carefully.

His days in Binger may seem a long way off now, but those who know Johnny Bench say success hasn't changed his basic personality at all. He's always been a quick-thinking leader, with the sensitivity to consider the feelings of others. And on the field he seems to be taking giant steps toward his self-proclaimed goal of being the greatest catcher ever to play the game.

4. Reggie Jackson

It was late July, 1971, all-star game time for major league baseball. The best players from the American and National Leagues were gathered in Detroit's Tiger Stadium for the 42nd annual midsummer classic.

The National Leaguers were loose and relaxed. Why not? The Senior Circuit was on an eight-game all-star win streak, and the big guns—Mays, Aaron, Clemente, Bench, Torre, etc.—were on hand once more to wreak havoc on the poor American Leaguers. And they usually did it with relish, since league rivalry and the question of superiority were always at stake.

For the American Leaguers, there was an air of desperation. Let's face it, they were downright embarrassed. They hadn't won this game in eight years, and most people had acknowledged that it was more than coincidence. The National League simply had the better players . . . any way you looked at it.

But the American League had an ace in the hole this time. They'd be starting Vida Blue, the young lefthander of the Oakland Athletics, who brought a dynamic, 17-3, record into the all-star game. Blue threw bullets, and had dazzled his opponents all year long. Now everyone figured he would do the same thing to the veteran sluggers from the N.L.

There was another member of the Oakland Athletics on the all-star squad, an outfielder, a last-minute selection when a starter was injured. His name was Reggie Jackson.

Just two years earlier, Jackson was the slugging sensation of the league. By the end of July in that 1969 season, he had hit 39 home runs and looked like a good bet to top Babe Ruth and Roger Maris. But he slumped that year and finished with 47 homers. The slump carried over to the entire 1970 season. In 1971, he was fighting his way back, having a good year, so the all-star selection made him happy.

More than 50,000 fans jammed Tiger Stadium on that July night, most of them waiting to see Vida Blue do a job on the cocky National Leaguers, while millions more gathered in front of TV sets all over the country.

Blue didn't disappoint anyone in the first inning. He threw just seven pitches, all fastballs, and retired Willie Mays, Hank Aaron and Joe Torre. None of them had gotten a good piece of the ball. But in the second inning, things changed.

Vida let one slip and it nicked Willie Stargell on the arm. The big Pirate slugger trotted to first and up stepped Johnny Bench. Bench was having an off year himself, but he timed a Blue fastball perfectly and drove a rocket deep into the second deck in left. Suddenly, the National Leaguers had a 2-0 lead. When old man Aaron homered off Blue in the third, making it 3-0, it looked like another National League rout.

The A.L. did nothing with the National's Dock Ellis in the first two frames. Then came the third. Luis Aparicio, batting in the eighth spot, singled to center. Blue was due up next. American League manager Earl Weaver decided to make a move. He motioned to Reggie Jackson to get up there and hit for his teammate.

Reggie dug in from the left side of the plate and wigwagged his bat out toward Ellis. The big righthander worked carefully to Jackson, mixing his fastball and curve. He had two strikes on the pinch hitter and figured he was in command. Then he tried to catch Reggie off guard with a fastball.

Around came the bat, followed by the unmistakable sound of solid contact. The ball left the box as if jet propelled. It rose majestically in the nighttime Detroit sky and headed to right centerfield. And it kept rising. Aaron and Mays each took a step, as if to converge on the drive, then stopped and watched. The ball was still rising when it sailed over the fence.

In fact, it not only cleared the fence, it cleared everything, and would have gone clear out of Tiger Stadium had it not hit a generator box at the top of the right tower in right center. The tower was more than 500 feet from home plate.

The huge crowd was stunned to silence by the magnitude of the drive. Most of the fans had never seen a ball hit so hard or so far. There's no telling how far it would have traveled if it hadn't hit the tower. Reggie circled the bases slowly, savoring the moment, then reached for the hands waiting for him at the dugout.

A shaken Ellis gave up a walk, then a more conventional homer to Frank Robinson, and the American League took the lead. A two-run shot by Harmon Killebrew later in the game put it on ice, and the A.L. finally had an all-star victory, 6-4.

After the game, almost all the talk centered on the home run hit by Reggie Jackson. Even the other players couldn't believe it.

"I can't remember seeing a ball hit that hard or that far," said Al Kaline, who plays regularly at Tiger Stadium. "Too bad it hit that thing up there. I would have loved to have seen where it ended up."

Former Yankee Tony Kubek, who was on the announcing team covering the game, said, "I've seen three other balls hit over the roof here, two by Mickey Mantle and one by Norm Cash. But this one seemed to be the hardest hit. I think it was still rising when it made contact out there."

And Johnny Bench, who hit a hard shot himself, commented, "I thought Reggie's drive was going to knock the whole tower down. I've never seen a ball take off that way."

A realistic note was added by Frank Robinson, who hit the homer behind Reggie's. "Reggie played for me in Puerto Rico this winter," Robby said, "and after watching him there I'm not in awe at all of what he did. He's got so much strength and ability that you knew something like this was bound to happen sooner or later."

As for 25-year-old Reggie Jackson, he tried to play the whole thing down. "I didn't want to strike out," he told reporters, "and I wasn't trying for a home run, really. I just tried to meet the ball, but I do think it was the longest one I've ever hit. And the people amazed me. They were dumbstruck. They just sat there. They didn't even cheer."

But when a reporter asked if Reggie got an extra charge out of hitting it, a bright gleam flashed in the youngster's eye.

"Sure I did," he said.

There have been a lot of high and low points in the career of Reggie Jackson. They've come and gone at almost regular intervals, like the tide. First the promise, then the letdown, next a period of brilliance, followed by one of decline. None of it set easy on the shoulders of this thinking, sensitive man, who, in his brief career, has been called the next Ruth one year, and threatened with demotion to the minor leagues the next. Sometimes the pressure and puzzlement have been so great that Reggie himself has contemplated retirement. Yet, today, as the acknowledged leader of the World Champion Oakland Athletics, Reggie Jackson still stands on the threshold of a bright future.

Reginald Martinez Jackson was born in Wyncote, Pennsylvania, a suburb of Philadelphia, on May 18, 1946. His father, Martinez C. Jackson, was of Spanish ancestry on his mother's side. When Reggie was still a tot, his family moved from Wyncote to Cheltenham, a rather high-class section, also near Philly. Reggie's father had a dry-cleaning delivery route there. But the family didn't stay together for long. When Reggie was four, his parents were divorced.

Three of his brothers and sisters went to live with their mother, Clara, while Reggie, an older brother and a sister stayed with their father. As a consequence, Reggie was on his own as a youngster, and had to learn to fend for himself at an early age.

Fortunately, the family didn't live in a tough neighborhood, where a solitary youth like Reggie could have fallen into bad company. "Cheltenham was a pretty rich place," Reggie said. "There were very few blacks in the neighborhood, but I guess there had to be someone to do the work.

"But I never felt much prejudice. Since I was the

only black, I guess there was more or less no need for it. And since that time, I've always been a well-known athlete, so that's helped keep me away from it, too. But I did know what it was like to be poor, especially since we were in such a rich place. Everyone around there had more than we did."

By most standards, Reggie didn't have a normal boyhood. He didn't have the benefit of a mother's love, and he didn't have much fun. It wasn't until he discovered sports that he really began to enjoy himself. But his boyhood made him more keenly aware of many things, and he's always given deep thought to the way people treat each other.

A street gang in Cheltenham was as rare as a snowball fight in July, and Reggie never fell into the trap that has ruined the lives of so many young boys who are missing a solid home life. He always had friends and for the most part they treated him very well. Since he was the best athlete, the other kids always wanted him on their side and would often covet his attention so he'd play with them. But that didn't remove the bleakness of his everyday routine.

"My dad was up and out of the house very early," Reggie explained, "so I had to get up, wash, get dressed, and get over to school by myself. I rarely ate any breakfast during the week because we didn't have much in the house. Dad didn't get home some nights until ten or eleven, and that's when we ate supper.

"There were a lot of tough times when he had to do anything he could to support us, but he always kept something on the table and we never starved. If I wanted a quarter to go to the movies or something, he'd always make me earn it. Sometimes I'd work on his delivery truck, but then it was too late for the movies anyway. My father was strict with me, but I respected him for it. He made me see the value of money."

Reggie was a ballplayer as soon as he reached elementary school and became involved in competition. Bob Tremble, now the athletic director at Cheltenham High, knew Reggie from the time he was a third grader and coached the youngster during the early days.

"It might sound hard to believe," Tremble said, "but Reggie Jackson was always a terrific kid, right from the time I first knew him. He never caused any trouble and always had a lot of friends. He was nice to everyone around him and they enjoyed his company.

"Reggie was always a good ballplayer, too. You could see the speed and good hands right from the first. In fact, when he was in the fifth grade, I tried making him a switch hitter. He practiced that way for a while, then went back to the left side.

"One thing I noticed about him even then was his willingness to help others. When he was in the fifth and sixth grades, he was helping the younger kids. He'd play catch with them, or throw passes to them, and show them the various skills he'd learned from me. I've really got nothing but good things to say about Reggie Jackson."

Reggie the ballplayer continued to stand out right through junior high. When he entered his sophomore year at Cheltenham High in 1961, he was ready to play ball.

"Reggie was a star for three years," said his baseball coach at Cheltenham, Chuck Mehelich. "He had tremendous potential, even as a sophomore. I'd just have to call him an exceptional all-around athlete. He was an outfielder on the baseball team, a running back and defensive back on the football squad, and high jumped and ran sprints with the track team.

"He started in the outfield for me as a sophomore. He had great speed and a great arm, and he hit well. There were no fences at most of the schools, and the other teams played him way back, so he didn't get many homers that year, but plenty of singles, doubles and triples. His arm was so strong that he pitched some relief for us, too. I remember one practice game when he struck out 17 batters in 12 innings. I think he could have made the grade as a pitcher if he wanted to."

By the time he reached his junior year, Reggie was a star. He was the only black on both the football and baseball teams, yet once again he met with no prejudice, getting along well with everyone. He had many friends at Cheltenham and enjoyed his time there. Academically, he stayed in the upper third of his class and was considered a bright student.

And all the while he was improving as a ballplayer. As a junior on the unbeaten Cheltenham football team, Reggie averaged about eight yards per carry from his halfback slot and scored a bevy of touchdowns. Then in the final game he got racked up.

"Reggie was in a real pileup," recalls Chuck Mehelich. "I don't know how many pounds of beef jumped on him, but when they picked him up he had several bruised vertebrae in his neck. It was a serious injury and he was forced to wear a neck brace for a good number of weeks. To tell you the truth, I thought he was through. But when baseball practice started, there was Reggie, and he wasn't holding back a bit. He went all out, as usual, right from the start.

"I remember one big game we had that year. We were losing it, 4-1. Reggie had already struck out three times on change-ups. He really had trouble hitting the off-speed pitches. Anyway, when he came up again, we had the bases loaded. It was our last chance.

"Well, Reggie ran the count to three and two, and I was about to get an ulcer. So I asked for time and called him over. 'Do the team a favor,' I told him. 'Don't try to kill the ball. Take a half cut and just meet it.' He said OK and went back up.

"Sure enough, the pitcher threw a change-up and Reggie just seemed to flick his bat at it. Well, he belted that thing over the rightfielder's head and over seven parked cars. I think it was still rolling when he crossed home plate. All on a half swing."

The Cheltenham team was 13-3 that year and won the Southern League title. As for Reggie, he hit well over .300, and cracked about six of those long, rolling homers. And to the surprise of no one, before the year was over, some veteran baseball scouts bgan nosing around the Cheltenham practice sessions.

One of them was Hans Lobert, a Giants scout who followed Reggie for two years. Willie Mays was always the young slugger's idol, and he thought about playing for the Giants. But the Pirates, Phils, Twins and Dodgers were also interested, and Reggie still had a year to play it cool.

"Reggie got racked up again at the end of his junior year," said Chuck Mehelich. "We were practicing late one night and Reggie asked one of the pitchers to throw to him. He said he wanted the pitches in tight. Well, he lost sight of the ball and it cracked him right in the jaw.

"I thought at first that it caught him in the temple. He wasn't wearing a protective helmet and I saw blood spurting out of his mouth. I carried him about 600 feet to my car and rushed him to the hospital. The doctors found that his jaw was broken in three places.

"They wired the jaw and sent him home. Well, I think the wire lasted about three days. That's when he got sick of it and removed it himself. He was right back in school and made a speedy recovery. And the amazing part is, that as soon as he began playing baseball again, he dug right in there. He wasn't gun shy in the least."

Reggie continued his hot pace as a senior and knew the time was coming for him to make a decision. The scouts were still hanging around, but their offers didn't exactly make Reggie drool. At the same time, some 48 colleges were offering him scholarships as a footballer. Since he wasn't completely sold on a baseball career, he and his father agreed that by attending college, he might raise his market value in both sports.

The scholarship offers were more than nickel-and-dime stuff. And the schools weren't exactly Podunk, either. Notre Dame, Penn State, Syracuse and Michigan State were among the colleges bidding for his gridiron talents. Reggie was no slouch with the pigskin.

Schools like Dartmouth and George Washington were offering the same thing, but for baseball. Then along came Arizona State to say he could play both sports.

"That's what Reggie really wanted," Chuck Mehelich said. "He had a football scholarship with an eye to baseball. Arizona State played about fifty or sixty games a year, so he could really have a complete season. That's where he decided to go."

When Chuck Mehelich looks back at Reggie Jackson, he does so with affection and admiration. "Reggie was a great kid to have at school. He was extremely coachable and he wasn't a glory boy. He would do what you told him, and was always ready to sacrifice personal achievement for the good of the team. You only get one like him every ten or fifteen years. I'll never forget him."

So the youngster from the mainline Philadelphia suburb packed his bags and headed for the wide open spaces of Tempe, Arizona. It was autumn, 1964.

Reggie was a running back for the Sun Devil freshmen most of the season, until he sustained a knee injury that sidelined him for several games. He was already behind another back, and the knee injury settled things. When he returned, they made him a defensive back for good.

But his brief fling on offense netted him some fine statistics. As a freshman, he carried the ball 21 times for 161 yards, a fine 7.7 yards-per-carry average. He also grabbed seven passes for 98 yards. On defense, he was a hard-nosed tackler and good ballhawk. He looked like a fine varsity prospect no matter where he played.

The provisions of his scholarship said he couldn't play baseball his freshman year, but he worked out with the varsity at least twice a week during the spring. That's when he met Arizona State baseball coach Bobby Winkles, who is now the manager of the California Angels.

"Reggie was playing spring football that year," Winkles recalls, "and he just worked out with us on Tuesdays and Saturdays. He always brought his football bumps and bruises with him and looked pretty much banged up all the time.

"I knew he was a great prospect and would really help our club. We had Sal Bando, Rick Monday and Duffy Dyer that year, but I had a hunch a couple of them might sign and leave after the season, so I really looked forward to getting Reggie full time the next year.

"Right away you could see that he had tremendous power. When he connected, the ball took off . . . man, it really took off. But he did have a problem making contact consistently, and off-speed pitches really seemed to give him trouble. He had a tendency to lunge and jump at a pitch. And when he'd lunge at an off-speed job, he'd be way out ahead of it with no chance to time it right.

"Monday had the same problem when he came here. I used to tell them both not to stride until they saw the ball leave the pitcher's hand."

Winkles' hunch was right. When the 1965 baseball season ended, both Bando and Monday signed big bonus contracts with the Kansas City Athletics and left school. Reggie returned and played another season with the Sun Devil gridders, starting at defensive safety and playing well. Then, in the spring, he was ready to take over Monday's old centerfield spot with the baseball team.

"Reggie wasn't much of a fielder when he worked out with us as a freshman," Bobby Winkles said. "He always had that great arm, but some fly balls gave him trouble and he didn't always know what to do out there. But you've got to remember that we have a very high sky in Arizona. I've always said it's the toughest place in the world to catch a fly ball. But Reggie worked at it and he improved rapidly."

Once the season started, it quickly became obvious that Reggie Jackson was a college superstar. He became the power man in the Sun Devil attack, and his blazing speed on the basepaths and in the outfield dazzled the Arizona State fans and impressed outsiders who came to see the team play. Among those impressed were several big league scouts, including Bob Zuk of the Kansas City A's.

"I watched Reggie play in about 10 or 11 games that year," Zuk recalled, "and my opinion of him never changed. Sure, he might have had a bad game every now and then, but that happens to the big leaguers, too. I felt that Reggie had both the physical and mental equipment to make it . . . in fact, I thought he had the potential to be a superstar."

Reggie continued to smack the ball with authority. He still had some problems with the off-speed pitch, but on the whole his hitting was solid. As an outfielder, he was much improved, and his rifle arm gunned down runners who tried to take the extra base on him. Then, during a game in Albuquerque, he had a fielding lapse and dropped two flies. Coach Winkles wanted to shake him up so in the next game he batted Reggie ninth, instead of his customary fourth.

An angered Jackson belted a long homer to right his first time up. The next time he whacked a double down the rightfield line. The third time it was another double, this one to right center. "I decided right there that Reggie would be back in the fourth spot," said Winkles, "but he wasn't through yet."

When Reggie came up again, he pickled a hanging curve for his second homer. Then batting for a fifth time, he slammed a long triple between the astounded outfielders. Besides the five extra base hits, he had seven runs batted in on the day. It was more than obvious that Reggie Jackson was the real thing.

By the time the 1966 season ended at Arizona State, Reggie had firmly established himself as one of the top major league prospects in the country. In 52 games, he had come to bat 202 times, banging out 66 hits for a .327 average. But it was in the power department that he really excelled. He had nine doubles, six triples and a school record 15 homers. He also scored 56 runs and drove in 65. On the basepaths he was electric, stealing 15 times, and his strong arm in the outfield accounted for 10 assists. His only negative statistic was the 62 times he struck out during the course of the season.

"Reggie was just a great kid to have around," explained Bobby Winkles. "He was never too busy to help someone, especially athletes who were in trouble for breaking training or something like that. He didn't like people who looked down on others, and he always lectured at junior high and high schools, telling kids to stick with it and work hard. And he worked hard at many instructional clinics for kids, and never got a dime for it.

"He was admired and respected by all his teammates. He didn't smoke or drink, and he was a gentleman. Reggie was such an intense competitor that he sometimes got down on himself, but he wasn't the type you shouted at or insulted. With Reggie, you just had to sit down and talk things out, man to man, and that usually snapped him out of it."

By the end of the season, it was apparent that Reggie was becoming a hot commodity. And that's what he had had in mind when he decided to attend college. The new free agent draft system was in its second year, and that meant that he had to negotiate with the team that picked him. No longer could several teams bid for his services at once.

When Reggie found out that the team was the A's, he was happy. He knew that former Arizona State players Bando and Monday were already in the organization. It seemed like an up-and-coming team. Scout Bob Zuk began making offers, starting at $60,000. When it reached the area of $95,000, Reggie said yes. He was now a pro.

"I wasn't happy to lose a ballplayer and fine young man like Reggie," said coach Winkles. "But it was the best move for him and I advised him to sign. He was always a good student here and he's continued his education. He lives in Tempe during the off season and I believe he's very close to getting his degree right now."

As a sophomore at Arizona State, Reggie was named to the All-Western Athletic Conference, All-NCAA District Seven and College All-American first teams. He was also the first college player ever to hit a ball out of Phoenix Municipal Stadium, belting one close to 500 feet, and he was a prime mover in the team's solid, 41-11, record. It was a brief but outstanding college career.

There was still plenty of time left in the regular 1966 baseball season when Reggie left Arizona in early June. Bob Zuk recommended that Reggie be assigned to Lewiston, Idaho, a Class A team in the Rookie League. "I felt Reggie lacked confidence and should start in a place where he could handle the pitching," Zuk said.

It took Reggie just 12 games to handle the pitching at Lewiston. He cracked out 14 hits, seven of them for extra bases, including two homers, and he drove in 11 runs. The A's quickly sent him to Modesto, a Class A team in the California League.

Reggie played in 56 games at Modesto in 1966, batting .299, with 21 homers among his 66 hits. He drove in 60 runs and scored 50. But he was still a free swinger, striking out 71 times. The A's tended to overlook this. They felt Reggie was on his way, and perhaps they listened to Bobby Winkles, who once said of the Jackson swing, "You can't try to curb it. Just let him go. You'll never stop a guy with natural strength, and Reggie has an abundance of it."

Most of the 1967 season was spent at Birmingham in the Southern League, where Reggie hit .293, whacked 17 homers, and drove in 58 runs. In addition, he had an amazing total of 17 triples, a further tribute to his speed and baserunning ability. He played the game full tilt, and with uncontrolled abandon. After appearing in 114 games for Birmingham that year, he was brought up to Kansas City for his first shot. And when he arrived in K.C., he learned he had been named Southern League Player of the Year.

In 35 games with Kansas City at the tail end of the 1967 season, Reggie was wild and undisciplined. He was a bit awed at being in the majors at 21, and there wasn't really enough time for him to settle into any kind of good groove, especially since he didn't know whether he'd be playing every day or not.

He came to bat 118 times that year, collecting just 21 hits, only one homer, and driving in six runs. His batting average was a miniscule .178, and his free swinging produced 46 strikeouts. Yet after the season, the management of the A's admitted they liked what they saw.

"Reggie Jackson has tremendous ability and potential," a club spokesman said at a news conference. "We're expecting big things from him in the future. Yes, we expect him to be the regular rightfielder next season."

Then there was another announcement. Charlie O. Finley, the team's owner, had just received permission from the American League to move his team from Kansas City to Oakland, California. The A's would be heading for the glamour of the West Coast, and they were telling newsmen of the club's potential, running down the roster of young, exciting players.

Besides Reggie, there were his predecessors at Arizona State, Sal Bando and Rick Monday, giving the A's one of the best trios of youngsters in the league. Although the team had finished last in '67, with a 62-99 record, there was plenty of optimism for the future. The pitching looked to be improving, and the farm system was beginning to produce better quality players.

So the A's went West and as predicted, Reggie Jackson had a good spring and was the starting rightfielder opening day. The young Oakland players were maturing on schedule, and the team was no longer the league patsy it had been for so many years.

As for Reggie, he was both brilliant and brutal, putting on a display of inconsistency that had him headed for the Hall of Fame one day and oblivion the next. It wasn't unusual for him to hit a titanic home run, then strike out four times. Or he might stretch a single to a double with his blinding speed, then try it again when he should have stopped at first.

Sometimes he gunned down runners with an arm as powerful as anyone's, but then he'd uncork a throw that would clear the base by 20 feet. He made brilliant, unbelievable catches in the outfield, but also misjudged easy flies, and even got hit on the head by one. Another time he tried a basket catch, à la Willie Mays, and it backfired on him.

There were days when the fans loved him, and days when they jeered him unmercifully. The press praised and condemned him alternately, and his teammates also waxed hot and cold in their relations with him.

One night, late in the year, he popped up against the Yanks with runners on base. As soon as he saw where the ball was going, he turned around and pounded his bat on the ground, breaking it in half. When questioned about his rookie's actions by a newsman, Oakland manager Bob Kennedy said:

"Reggie's just a kid who's trying to find himself. Just have patience with him. When he realizes just how good he can be, watch out. He's really gonna be something."

When the 1968 season ended, Reggie's statistics indicated the inconsistency. He had played in 154 games, so he was surely a regular. In 553 trips to the plate he made 138 hits for .250 average. Not bad. He also clubbed 29 homers and drove in 74 runs. Also pretty good for a rookie. But he struck out a fantastic 171 times, coming within four whiffs of the major league record. Observers said he sometimes flailed away at pitches over his head or in the dirt. He made 18 errors in the outfield, but still had 14 assists. And he stole 14 bases.

After the season, there was plenty written and said about the young slugger, and much of it was as inconsistent as his play.

One writer said, "When he's (Reggie) on a hot streak he swells up and won't give you the time of day, but when he's not going good, he goes out of his way to look for friends." Yet another said, "Reggie's happy when he's hot and nasty when he's cold."

Then one of his teammates commented: "The guy can't control his temper. It ties him up in knots and holds him back." But conversely, another Oakland player commented, "Sometimes I think he doesn't care about anything. He doesn't seem to have the desire to reach all that potential he has."

It was puzzling, all right, but Reggie stood right up and answered his critics.

"When I was in college," he said, "I had a coach who stressed sportsmanship and hustle. He taught me to control my anger, not to curse and show my temper. Then one day at Modesto, I remember I struck out and hustled back to the dugout like I did in college. Well, some guy starts getting on me, saying the least I could do was act as if I cared up there. Most of them cursed, threw their helmets, kicked things . . . that kind of stuff. Soon I found myself doing it again.

"Then there was that time last year when I broke my bat at Yankee Stadium. No sooner did that happen when some of the veterans started lecturing me on how I couldn't expect to hit a homer and make a great catch every time. They said I had to accept the strikeouts and the errors. So I began to cool it again and what happens . . . people start with the same old stuff about me not caring."

Then he added, "Let me tell you something. I care. But sometimes I tend to hold things back until I finally explode. I haven't made friends easily up here and I've found it difficult to confide in people. And there are so many people telling me what to do that I just don't know who to listen to. I've just got to get a better grip on myself and I think it will happen as I get older."

The second major criticism of Reggie's play was his unusually high number of strikeouts. He felt compelled to talk about that, too.

"I'm a long ball hitter," he said, "and most long ball hitters strike out a lot. I think I have a good swing, a natural swing, and I take it, even with two strikes on me. That doesn't mean I'm overswinging. Sure, I've gone after some bad balls, but that should go with more experience. I've got to learn not to be overanxious. But I've also got to be aggressive at the plate and I don't plan to stop attacking the ball. I'm just not going to worry about striking out.

"Look at it this way. Frank Howard and Rich Allen both strike out a lot and they're in the money. I remember reading about Allen striking out four times in a game this year and it was the tenth or eleventh time he'd done that in his career. And how about Mantle? He always struck out a lot and he makes a hundred grand a year. It seems to me that they pay off on homers, not strikeouts."

Reggie's fierce pride prevented him from giving much ground on any of the issues. He was well aware of the parts of his game that needed improvement and he was determined to work on them. But he wouldn't take the criticism sitting down.

One person who showed some compassion for Reggie's problem was Joe DiMaggio, the famed Yankee Clipper, who was at that time an Oakland vice president and special batting coach. "You can't just go to someone and say don't swing as hard," explained DiMag, "because when that guy sees the ball coming up to the plate, he figures he can hit it out and he's gonna take his natural cut at it.

"Let's face it, it's an unusual thing when a ballplayer swings at nothing but strikes. Still, when a batter has two strikes on him, he's got to learn to protect that plate. And he can't possibly have his best swing if he's looking for a certain pitch."

A veteran Detroit pitcher, Earl Wilson, explained his own ideas on Reggie's problem. "He just doesn't know the strike zone yet," said Wilson, "and I'm sure glad he doesn't. Because if he did, he'd really hurt somebody."

Reggie hurt plenty of people in 1968, despite all his problems. He belted 400-foot-plus homers off the likes of Dean Chance, Rick Clark and Mike Paul, all three shots winning one-run games. He also hit a mammoth homer off the Yanks' Steve Barber, and belted a 490-foot drive off lefty Clyde Wright of the Angels. Against each of the top teams—Detroit, Baltimore, and Minnesota—Reggie had 10 RBI's. He had 15 against the Yankees. And he rose to the occasion more than once during the season.

Early in the year, veteran Hoyt Wilhelm tied Cy Young's record for the most pitching appearances in a career. Reggie picked out a Wilhelm knuckler that day and sent it to the downs. Then, late in the season, Denny McLain faced Oakland on national television.

It was a big game since McLain was bidding to become the majors' first 30-game winner in more than 35 years. All Reggie did that day was belt two homers, make a brilliant catch, and gun down a runner at home plate. In the final game of the season he clubbed a two-run homer against Minnesota in a futile bid to give the A's a first division, fifth-place finish.

As it was, the Oakland team surprised everyone, surging to an 82-80 mark and finishing sixth in the 10-team loop. Reggie's heroics played a big part in the resurgence. That was one of the points he made when he asked for a larger contract in the spring of 1969. Charlie Finley offered him $18,000; he wanted $23,000. When Finley said no, Reggie Jackson's first holdout began.

While still standing on the sidelines waiting for his contract dispute to be settled, Reggie talked of the furor and frustrations of his first season in the big leagues. Maybe it was just talk, but he began on a very negative-sounding note.

"I don't really have to play baseball," he said. "Sure, I want to play, but if I'm not wanted enough around here, there are other things I can do.

"I know I've had a really good first year when you take everything into consideration, and I have a great chance to have a fine career. I want it. But baseball isn't all home runs and glory, and picking up a fat paycheck. There are all the times you strike out, or throw a big one away. Sometimes you get so mad at yourself that you can't see straight. Then there's all those plane rides and living out of suitcases, and sitting around hotel lobbies until you can't tell one from the other.

"I love the games, but think about all the other hours you spend at the ballpark, every day, seven days a week, seven months a year. There's so much pressure and it can wear you down. I'm 21 years old and I got tired last year. I mean mentally tired. Sometimes it's hard for me to understand those guys who love every minute of it and never let up. I think they're a little flaky, maybe a little crazy. I respect them, but I can't be like them. I can only be what I am, whatever that is."

Reggie's despondence was clear in his comments. Many have testified that when he's on the field, there's no fiercer competitor in all of baseball. He plays the game hard and he wants to win. When he finally came to terms with the A's in the spring of 1969 (for about $22,000), he worked to get in shape and started the season smoking.

By the time the schedule was just a few weeks old, it had become apparent that the six-foot, 195-pound second-year man was intent on tearing the league apart with his bat. He was still taking the big swing, but this time rocketing the ball out of the park and making contact more often.

By June 1, Reggie had belted 16 home runs and had a slugging percentage of .713. He wasn't striking out as much and his all-around play was much improved and more consistent. His college coach, Bobby Winkles, saw him in action and said, "Reggie is already a much better ballplayer than I thought he'd be at this stage."

His pre-season holdout was already forgotten and he was being showered with praise from everyone connected with the team, including owner Charles Finley. American League pitchers tried everything to stop him but couldn't. During May, the A's went up against Detroit. Pitching was Earl Wilson, the big righthander who said that Reggie didn't know the strike zone as a rookie, but lived in fear of his learning it.

The count went to two strikes. Wilson tried to slip one by on the outside corner. The old Jackson would have taken a big riffle and missed it. But the 1969 Reggie just flicked his bat out and lined a hit to leftfield.

"He never used to do that," Wilson commented after the game. "I tried to throw a slider past him and make him think the pitch was a ball. But he reached out and got it. I really don't like throwing to him. He's always a threat to hit the ball out of the park."

Reggie was more than a threat in 1969. By all-star game time he had clubbed a fantastic 39 home runs, and he was running some 25 or so games ahead of Babe Ruth's famous 60-home-run pace. He was putting together an amazing season, and there was speculation that he'd finish with between 65-70 homers. Though he wouldn't come out with any predictions, Reggie was totally enjoying his new-found success.

"No problem with a temper this year," he said. "But I must admit that it's a lot easier to live at the top than down at the bottom.

"It's funny, but I always thought tipping your cap to the fans was a hot-dog play. But after I hit a homer and trot around the bases, I'd just like to stop at home plate and let the fans serenade me with their cheers. I really learned to love them. In fact, I almost suggested to Mr. Finley to have a game where everyone was let in free."

Reggie started in the all-star game that year, was hitless in two trips, then went back to the business of trying to help his team to a pennant. The A's were greatly improved all around. Bando and Monday seemed to be coming into their own, and the Arizona State trio, along with some talented young pitchers and a buzz-bomb shortstop, Bert Campaneris, had the team challenging the veteran Minnesota Twins for the American League Western Division crown.

There were unending heroics for Reggie in the first half of the season. In one game he belted three homers and drove in 10 runs. As he circled the bases for the third time, Finley stood up in his box near the A's dugout and bowed ceremoniously to his young slugger. Yet Charlie O. reminded his manager, Hank Bauer, to keep Reggie under wraps, and the tough ex-marine let Reggie know whenever he made a mistake. Reggie took it well, saying, "I guess my bosses don't want me getting too big for my britches."

But shortly after the all-star break, the bubble burst. It almost had to. The pace was just too fantastic. The American League pitchers were getting tired of craning their necks to watch Reggie's long home runs sailing over distant fences. Before long, they were throwing him curveballs, working around the corners, and not worrying about it if he walked.

One reporter covering the team said, "It was amazing, but almost a whole week would go by without anyone throwing Reggie a fastball or even a decent pitch to hit. If they did throw the fastball, it was a waste pitch, a setup for the curve. I don't know how he stood it."

After belting 39 homers through July, Reggie hit only eight more the rest of the way. It wasn't only the pitchers. He just lost the magic. Part of it was a good old-fashioned slump. It almost had to happen.

"I knew what the pitchers were doing," Reggie said. "But I'm a home run hitter and I have to swing big. I'm learning more about the pitchers with each game. I know I'll begin to hit more homers off curveballs, then I'll see the fastballs again. Most sluggers don't reach their peaks until they're about 30. So that gives me another six years or so to learn. And I think my all-around play has improved greatly since I've been there."

Then he added, "I've always been a slow starter. This year I got off to a great start, but then hit a pretty bad slump. Still, being a slow starter can get you down, so I'm glad I got off well. You just have to learn to weather the bad times until the good times come along.

"I guess you could say I'm a ballplayer who plays like the rain. Rain is something you know is coming, but you just don't know exactly when. The superstars are like the sun. They come up every day. With guys like Aaron, Mays or Billy Williams, the only question is how hot they're gonna be."

But no one could criticize Reggie's season when it finally ended. He was instrumental in bringing the A's to a second-place finish. The team had a mark of 88-74, finishing behind the Twins in their division.

Reggie ended up with 47 homers, ranking third in the league. But he led the league in runs scored with 123 and in intentional walks with 24. All told, A.L. pitchers walked him 114 times. He also had 36 doubles, three triples, 118 runs batted in and a solid batting average of .275. His strikeout total was down to 142, and he had shown the baseball world his tremendous potential. Yet at the same time he was putting pressure on himself to better his own achievements.

It was a busy off-season for him. He lived in Tempe, Arizona, and was going into real estate and land developing. His great season put him in demand for dinners, speaking engagements and other personal appearances. Yet he came to spring training in 1970 eager to get started once again.

That's when the trouble began. It was an old story. His holdout prior to the 1969 season had resulted in about a $22,000 contract. Finley offered him $40,000. Reggie balked. He wanted $60,000. The two sides exchanged words. Camp opened. For the second straight year, Reggie Jackson was officially a holdout.

The bickering continued. Soon it became a heated battle. Two weeks passed, then four, then six. Reggie still hadn't signed. He was losing valuable training time and he knew it. Finley had some sound arguments. He went back to the big bonus Reggie had been paid and felt that it should be taken into consideration. Plus the A's still had not won a pennant and the fans in the Bay City were slow to accept their new team. What it boiled down to was his feeling that Reggie wanted too much too soon. Finley wanted patience and loyalty.

"Maybe I am asking too much," Reggie said one day.

"I'm sure everyone has an opinion. But it's not too much when you look at what some other guys in baseball are getting for lesser accomplishments. And it's not a matter of seniority. If I had five or six seasons like last year I'd be in the $100,000 class. Unfortunately, I have no choice over what team has the right to me and I can't move on. If they can't afford to pay me, why don't they trade me to a team that can?"

No luck, Finley wasn't about to trade anyone of Reggie's ability, nor was he going to squander a ballplayer who represented a major investment to him. And Reggie was also the A's biggest drawing card at the time. Finley needed him, but he wasn't about to cater to him.

The holdout went into the seventh week, then Reggie signed. The terms were disclosed as $47,000 base pay, and season-long rent on a $400-a-month apartment in Oakland.

"Sure I felt like I'd given in," Reggie told a newsman. "But there was certainly an obligation on my part. I owed it to the guys to report and I wanted to play baseball. I just didn't have much time to get in shape."

That was the problem. When the season started, Reggie was seven weeks behind everyone else, and his performance showed it. His timing was off and he looked bad at the plate. The A's hoped to get off the mark quickly in what was expected to be another close battle with Minnesota, and they needed their big man to do it.

But Reggie wasn't producing. Soon word filtered out of Oakland that he was benched. John McNamara was the A's new manager in 1970, but it was apparent that orders for the benching came right from the top, from Charles O. Finley.

"Reggie has worked hard to get in shape this spring, I know that," Finley said. "But he doesn't have his timing yet and he hasn't been aggressive enough at the plate, especially against lefthanded pitchers. I can't say he's really been helping the club. And if he doesn't start hitting at least righthanders, he might have to go down to the minors to get it back."

It was another low point for Reggie, maybe the lowest ever. Finley's last remark was especially cutting, and when Reggie heard it, he snorted, "Harmon Killebrew isn't doing much better than I am. I wonder if they're going to send him to the minors?"

For a short time, Reggie was used solely as a pinch runner and late-inning defensive substitution. He did hit a homer off a lefty in a rare start, but then he was benched again. He was growing bitter.

"I don't think I did anything wrong," he said. "I just tried to get the best possible contract for myself. Except for last year, I've always been a slow starter. They ought to know that. And even if they wanted to bench me for a few days, I think I deserve a second chance. Even the players are kidding me about being the game's only $50,000 pinch runner. Maybe they all expect too much of me. I'm just 24 now. Who do they think I should be, Henry Aaron?"

So Reggie continued to sit the bench. There were rumors of big offers for him from other teams. But Finley said with finality, "I won't trade him!" To which Reggie promptly answered, "If he has so much money invested in me, how can he let me go to waste?"

The battle of words continued and Reggie stayed on the bench. Like his career so far, his moods hit a series of alternate peaks and valleys.

"I'll tell you something," he said. "There's nothing better than hitting a ball hard, real hard. Just the feel of it, the sound of it, everything. It's beautiful. And I love going to the ballpark, putting on that uniform, then playing in front of a packed house. There's nothing like it."

But at other times he'd be down and he'd say, "I never wanted to be an overnight sensation. I wanted to progress steadily until I realized my full potential. I always thought I was with a progressive organization that was building a championship team, a team that was so strong it could roll over other teams the way the Orioles do. Now I find myself dreaming of playing somewhere else, a place where I can play in peace and maybe have the chance to be the player I should be.

"I don't want to give all this up, but the few years I've been in baseball are slowly breaking my spirit. A lot of the joy has gone out of the game for me. I should be on the threshold of my best years, but instead I find myself thinking of leaving the game."

Then sometimes he became downright philosophical. "I've got to keep this whole thing in perspective. For instance, there are some 400 million people starving in India. How many of them care if I'm hitting .190?"

It was a more cautious, restrained Reggie Jackson who waited for his chance to get back in the lineup. He was quiet, stopped talking to most of the writers and tried not to play up any conflicts with Charles O. Finley.

"There was a time I said I couldn't understand guys who went out and hustled every single game, day after day for seven months," he said. "But it's funny, the more the game's taken away from me, the more I want it."

It wouldn't be right to say that it was a new Reggie Jackson emerging from the ruins. He always hustled, but he was realistic enough to recognize the bad sides of baseball. Now he just had to put all that somewhere in the back of his mind and concentrate on playing the game.

By mid-June, Reggie had regained his starting job, against both right- and lefthanders. He patiently tried to break the long slump, containing his swing and playing the best team ball he could. The A's still trailed Minnesota, and Reggie still floundered below the .250 mark. But he was contributing.

The A's fell short again in 1970, finishing with an 89-73 mark and losing the title to the Twins once more.

As for Reggie, he emerged with the poorest statistical season of his short career. Playing in 149 games, he came to bat just 426 times, collecting 101 hits for a .237 average. In the power department he produced just 23 homers and 66 RBI's. The only area where he showed marked improvement was on the basepaths as he registered 26 steals.

During the offseason, Reggie tried to get his head together for a big comeback effort in 1971. He knew he wouldn't have salary problems, unless it was resisting the pay cut Finley was bound to ask him to take. But he wanted to be ready, so he decided to play winter ball in Puerto Rico. There, he found himself playing for a manager named Frank Robinson.

With Robinson giving the youngsters constant encouragement, Reggie began to get his timing back, and along with it, the good stroke. He was relaxed and enjoying the game of baseball completely. And playing for Robinson was a pure pleasure.

"If I could just walk in that man's image it would be tremendous," Reggie said. "I won't tell you he's God or a saint, but he's the best I've ever seen. He just told me, 'Reggie, with the ability you have, just go out there and play the game. I guarantee you'll have a good season.' I think he'll make a tremendous manager someday, and he's one guy I like to play against because he's a ballplayer's ballplayer."

The veteran Robinson saw the tremendous potential of young Jackson. "Nothing he does on the field will ever surprise me," Robby said. "He's got a world of talent, and he lives, eats and sleeps the game of baseball. All he needed was a little pat on the back."

Along with Reggie's new-found confidence and improved attitude, and his early entrance to spring training, something else happened with the A's in 1971 that was destined to help Reggie more than most people knew. It was the emergence of lefthander Vida Blue as the most exciting, charismatic performer in all of baseball.

Blue burst on the American League scene throwing bullets past bewildered hitters. He won game after game in the early going, striking out a host of batsmen and throwing goose eggs at the best teams in the league. A fastballing lefthander in the Sandy Koufax tradition, Blue caught the imagination of baseball people everywhere. They all wanted to see and hear young Vida.

Suddenly, everyone else around the Oakland clubhouse became expendable as far as the press and media were concerned. And the fans, too, had a new favorite in the young southpaw from Louisiana. In essence, what this did for Reggie Jackson was to make him Reggie Who?

A few years earlier, the lack of attention might have bothered young Reg, but not now. His troubles of the past seasons had been overpublicized, and he welcomed the chance to make his comeback attempt without excessive press coverage. There were no spring hassles and Reggie was in the opening day lineup in rightfield.

Another change in Oakland that year was the appointment of Dick Williams as the new manager. Williams took over on the final day of the 1970 season. Now he was starting his first full year. Williams was known as a no-nonsense type who expected one hundred percent from his ballplayers. He had piloted the Boston Red Sox to a pennant in 1967 and knew what it was like to finish on top. There were indications that owner Finley would let manager Williams run the club, one of Charlie O's failings with his other field bosses.

One of the first questions Williams was asked when he joined the A's was his opinion of Reggie Jackson.

"Well, you know that it was my Red Sox team that Reggie burned when he had those three homers and ten RBI's. I remember one of the homers he hit that day. It went into the right centerfield bullpen at Fenway

Park and was one of the hardest hit balls I've ever seen. You couldn't clap your hands twice before it landed. So I know what Reggie can do. I also know that he works hard and hustles all the time. He's got all the equipment to be great and I don't see why he shouldn't have a fine year."

Williams was right. While Blue continued to dazzle everyone, Reggie Jackson quietly reassumed leadership of the A's hitters. He was still having some of his old problems with the strikeout, but he was hitting with consistency and power. In the outfield, he was superb, making sure-handed catches and keeping runners honest with his powerful arm.

At all-star break time, the A's were solidly in first place. Blue was 17-3 and the talk of baseball. But in the all-star game, it was Reggie Jackson who stole the headlines with his mammoth pinch hit home run. Then some of the newsmen took a look at the stats.

Coming into the midseason game, Reggie Jackson was hitting a solid .272, with 17 home runs and 40 RBI's. Without much fanfare, he was getting the job done.

And that's the way it remained. Blue did not have a great second half, though still finishing with a 24-8 record. The A's wound up with an impressive 101-60 mark and swept to the A.L.'s Western Division title.

As for Reggie, he finally achieved the thing he always wanted—consistency. He finished the year with a .277 batting average, 32 home runs, and 80 runs batted in. It wasn't a super season such as he had in 1969, but it was solid. And his first and second half numbers were almost identical. He seemed to be on the way back.

"I found Reggie Jackson to be a hustling fool," said Dick Williams. "I was also impressed by his leadership ability. He never gives up out there, and the other guys respect and follow him. I know there were stories about his temper, but I didn't find any evidence of it. Of course, all outstanding players have the same problem.

The fans expect too much. But Reggie didn't get down at all during the season.

"And I think he's beginning to really mature as a hitter. He's been a better hitter with two strikes on him. He's learning to go with the pitch, and he's improved on off-speed pitches. He wants to learn all he can about the game and he wants to know how all the positions should be played."

In the 1971 championship playoff series, the A's went up against Baltimore for the right to enter the World Series. The Orioles were baseball's most powerful team and had rolled over the Twins in divisional playoffs the past two years. This time it was no different.

Vida Blue started the first game and held a 3-1 lead into the seventh inning. Then the Orioles erupted for four runs and went on to win it, 5-3. They had beaten the A's best pitcher. When Mike Cuellar bested Oakland's Catfish Hunter (another 20-game winner), 5-1, in the second game, it was all over. In game three, the Birds won again, 5-3, to eliminate the A's and move on to the Series.

In that final game, Reggie Jackson did all he could to keep his team in contention. The powerful slugger belted two long homers, but it wasn't good enough. Reggie had been outstanding in all three games, adding a double and single to his circuit shots for a .333 average. He played a great outfield and struck out only once. His 11 total bases were more than any other player on either team had compiled. When it was over, an Oakland newsman had this prediction:

"One by-product of this disastrous series has to be the re-emergence of Reggie Jackson as the A's leader. In each of the games against Baltimore, Reggie had the commanding presence of the superstar in residence. You could feel it, and you could sense the Birds were looking at him that way, too. It's the same way the A's view Frank Robinson—with a very definite respect.

"Reggie had a fine season in 1971. He didn't have the real big numbers, but he did the little things that characterize an outstanding ballplayer. Vida Blue got most of the attention, but Reggie did as much to help the team. He's the man they look up to now, and it should remain that way for a long time."

Dick Williams admired Reggie even more after managing him for a season. "Reggie Jackson is some kind of guy," the skipper said. "He'd give the shirt off his back to help someone. All year long he approached young players, advised them, coached them, helped them. Even rookies who didn't have much of a chance to make the club benefited from his help. He was never too busy to do all he could for them.

"Maybe it was some of the experiences he had before I got here, but he has more humility than any superstar I ever met. He knows he's not the only one on the team. But he loves playing the game and he wants to be the best at what he does. The result is that he makes all those around him go harder.

"As a ballplayer, he has awesome potential. I don't really know if he'll ever reach it, not because he doesn't want to, but because that potential is so great. He had an outstanding year in '71. You can't just judge it on the stats. It's the little things, like run production, advancing runners, playing team ball, taking the extra base. Reggie does it all."

Now that he seemed to be over the hump of inconsistency, Reggie relaxed. During the offseason he talked to reporters more openly. There were the nagging questions about his hitting, about his salary negotiations, about his moods. He was more himself, and he began to reveal his deeper thoughts and feelings.

One reporter noted that Reggie had a white roommate, pitcher Chuck Dobson, and many other good friends on the team who happened to be white. In fact, Reggie and Dobson requested to room together.

"Prejudice has eaten me alive," he said. He saw his

interviewer was surprised, and he quickly added, "Because of my background and my prominence as an athlete, I haven't really been exposed to it. But what has been directed to me and what I have seen has moved me to tears."

Another time, carefully choosing his words, Reggie said, "There have been some things I've said and done that I wish I could take back. I'm basically a thin-skinned person and afraid of being hurt. And I was always a loner. Now I think I pop off sometimes to keep people from getting too close to me. I've often hurt the feelings of people who mean quite a lot to me."

Intelligent, serious, sensitive. That's Reggie Jackson. He's painfully aware of the other things in life besides baseball. But once he's on the field, he gives everything to doing his job.

When 1972 rolled around, the A's talked about going all the way. They felt they had the personnel to do it. Then their chances were dealt a blow in the spring when Vida Blue and Charlie Finley couldn't get together on a contract. Blue held out, right into the season. It was all so similar to Reggie's situation of 1969-1970 that he must have known just what was going on in Vida Blue's mind.

But he had to play baseball. Fortunately, the team had traded for lefty Ken Holtzman, and he took up some of the pitching slack. The A's started quickly and jumped on top of their division. Despite a belated drive by the Chicago White Sox, Oakland really had no trouble repeating as A.L. West champs. The A's coasted home with a 93-62 record and their second straight divisional title.

Statistically, Reggie had another fine season, though his totals still fell short of the big year that he can't forget. But he missed 18 games at one stretch of 1972 and wound up playing in just 135 contests. He batted .265, with 25 homers and 75 RBI's. Plus he cut his strikeouts down to a career low of 125.

"As far as I'm concerned, Reggie Jackson had a superstar year," said Dick Williams. "He lost playing time to illness and injury, and that certainly cost him points on his batting average, and some homers and RBI's. You don't just step back into that good groove when you miss 18 games. And another thing, Reggie was a complete team player this year. When you play for the team, you lose points on your batting average, too, because you're always making sacrifices.

"Reggie did another thing that many people overlooked. We had some centerfield problems after we traded Monday. We tried a couple of players, but they couldn't work out. Then Reggie came to me and volunteered to go out there. Now I don't like taking an all-star rightfielder and putting him in another position. But we had to do it and Reggie was outstanding."

The A's were a close-knit, unique team in 1972. For one thing, they were the first baseball team to allow players the option of wearing hair on their face. Baseball has traditionally been the cleanest-cut of all the sports. While football players and basketball stars began wearing mustaches and beards, baseball resisted. But when it finally changed, Reggie Jackson was partly responsible.

"Reggie came to me in the spring of 1971," Dick Williams recalls. "He had a thick mustache at the time and he said to me that he'd shave it if I wanted him to. I said it didn't matter, he could do what he wanted. But I think he shaved it anyway.

"Then last year, he had the mustache again and a small beard. Again he asked me about it and again I said I didn't care. This time he kept it, and a few others started growing mustaches. Mr. Finley said he didn't mind, either, then he came up with a promotional gimmick, Mustache Day, held in mid-June. That's when the entire team, including myself, started growing them. Well, we kept them right through to the end of the year and I guess we began to look like we were right out of the gay nineties."

There's no doubt about the A's being baseball's most colorful team in '72. Finley's green-and-gold uniforms broke one drab tradition and the mustaches broke another. When the team entered the playoffs against the Detroit Tigers, many people were pulling for the Mustache boys to win.

It was a hard-fought series right from the start. Oakland won the first two games, 3-2, and 5-0, John Odom pitching the shutout. Then Detroit battled back. Joe Coleman blanked the A's, 3-0, and the Tigers rallied from the brink of defeat in the fourth game, getting two in the last of the tenth to win, 4-3. It came down to one last game, set for Detroit's Tiger Stadium, the same park where Reggie had hit his mammoth home run the year before.

Odom started for the A's against Woody Fryman of the Tigers. In the second inning, Reggie Jackson opened with a walk. With Bando up, Reggie broke for second. Catcher Bill Freehan's throw was on the mark, but the speedy Jackson slid under the tag. Safe.

Bando then lifted a fly to medium right. Reggie tagged, and again showed his speed by making it safely to third. Now big Mike Epstein was up. Fryman, unnerved by Reggie's daring on the basepaths, nicked Epstein with a pitch. The A's had runners on first and third.

Fryman looked in at the next hitter, got the signal and came to his stop. As he started his motion, Reggie broke for home plate, his spikes kicking up the dirt behind him. Freehan jumped out to get the ball. It arrived the same time as Reggie, who barreled in under the tag. He was safe again. He had stolen home to give his team a crucial lead.

Oakland players and fans went wild. But suddenly they stopped and looked out at home plate. Reggie wasn't getting up. He was lying on the ground in obvious pain, holding the back of his left leg. Everyone gathered around. He appeared to be hurt badly. Finally, he had to be helped from the field and removed from the game.

The A's went on to win it, 2-1, as Vida Blue came on to save the game for John Odom, giving Oakland its first American League championship. But even in victory, there was concern for Reggie Jackson. Hobbling on crutches and ready to go to the hospital for an examination, Reggie made his way to the Tiger dressing room to congratulate Detroit manager Billy Martin on a hard-fought series.

"You're one heck of a guy," Billy the Kid told Reggie. "Believe me, I don't like playing against you. You really showed me a lot of class. I like guys like you."

Reggie looked at the rest of the Tiger team. "I just came over to say that you fellows have a great amount of pride. Don't ever lose it."

Then he hobbled back to his dressing room. A reporter cornered him and asked him about Vida Blue, who had a 6-10 season after his long spring holdout that extended several weeks into the regular season. Reggie knew all about holdouts.

"I guess Vida went through about what I did. You know, you get to believing that you are the one person who is dominating all of baseball. It's hard to play well under those conditions, and I'd have to say that this was the first time all year that he was right mentally. But it couldn't have come at a better time."

Then they took Reggie to the hospital, and the diagnosis wasn't good. He had a badly torn hamstring muscle, and several other muscles in his leg were pulled out. He would definitely miss the World Series.

"I changed my slide just before I hit Freehan," he said. "It felt like someone reached inside my leg and just pulled everything apart. When I got to the clubhouse, I just started to cry.

"It's a rotten feeling to work your butt off all year

and then have this happen. But you just can't feel sorry for yourself forever. I've got to accept it. I'm hurt, I can't play and I can't help the team in the series.

"Of course, maybe if I hadn't scored that run we wouldn't have won the game. So in that respect it's worth it, almost an even trade. But I'd gladly give up my World Series share just for a chance to play."

Missing the Series hurt Reggie deeply. He couldn't help feeling he was letting the team down, though the injury certainly was no fault of his. And, of course, he was losing a chance to play in his first World Series.

"Reggie was very down about his injury," said manager Williams. "We decided to ask him to stay with the team on the bench, in his civilian clothes, and I think that's the first time someone's done that with an injured player. But he was introduced right along with the rest of us. And in the final game, I asked him to take the lineup cards to the plate. It was one way we could show him just how the team felt about him."

By now, the series is history. The A's went up against the powerful Cincinnati Reds, and without Jackson, were decisive underdogs. But it was the A's year. They won the first game, 3-2, on a pair of homers by second-string catcher Gene Tenace. Then Joe Rudi made an impossible catch against the leftfield wall at Cincinnati to save the second game, 2-1.

Cincy took the third behind the nifty pitching of Jack Billingham, 1-0, but Oakland won the fourth for a 3-1 lead. Just when it looked like it was over, Cincy bounced back. They took the fifth, then exploded for an 8-1 victory in the sixth. Playing in Cincinnati's Riverfront Stadium, Oakland was again the underdog in game seven.

Once again the hero was Tenace, who provided a key double as Oakland took it all, 3-2. The young catcher had four homers and nine RBI's in the series, and his surprising MVP play helped take up the power slack left by Jackson's absence.

When Pete Rose flied to Joe Rudi for the final out, the cameras panned the home plate area as the A's went wild in celebration. Charles O. Finley climbed on top of the Oakland dugout and began hugging and kissing his wife. He was soon joined by Dick Williams and his wife, and the Oakland fans who had journeyed from California cheered their leaders.

But those with sharp eyes caught another small drama being played out at home plate. The injured Reggie Jackson had come out on his crutches and was talking to Reds' catcher Johnny Bench at home plate. The two young superstars were good friends, and they spoke quietly, arms around each other's shoulders. The wounded gladiator and the losing gladiator, consoling each other and maybe planning an off-season get-together.

In a way, it was a very touching scene. The two young men, each about 25 years of age, one expected to be jubilant in victory, the other despondent in defeat. Yet they spoke quietly, almost detached from the bedlam around them. Both are fierce competitors, both have the drive and desire to go all out and play their hardest, every day. But both also have acquired the maturity to put their sport in perspective. Human communication was more important to them than uncontrolled emotion.

It's apparent that Reggie Jackson has finally climbed out of the valley for the last time. He has put together consecutive solid seasons, consistency now wearing the mantle that inconsistency had worn some years before. They were hard years. They weighed heavily on the sensitive young man from the Philadelphia suburb.

But Reggie Jackson is rolling now. He's the acknowledged leader of baseball's most colorful team. And he's widely recognized as one of the top all-around players in the game. Somehow, that's what Reggie always wanted.

Statistics

Hank Aaron

Year	Club	G	AB	R	H	2B	3B	HR	RBI	BA
1952	Eau Claire	87	345	79	116	19	4	9	61	.336
1953	Jacksonville	137	574	115	208	36	14	22	125	.362
1954	Milwaukee	122	468	58	131	27	6	13	69	.280
1955	Milwaukee	153	602	105	189	37	9	27	106	.314
1956	Milwaukee	153	609	106	200	34	14	26	92	.328
1957	Milwaukee	151	615	118	198	27	6	44	132	.322
1958	Milwaukee	153	601	109	196	34	4	30	95	.326
1959	Milwaukee	154	629	116	223	46	7	39	123	.355
1960	Milwaukee	153	590	102	172	20	11	40	126	.292
1961	Milwaukee	155	603	115	197	39	10	34	120	.327
1962	Milwaukee	156	592	127	191	28	6	45	128	.323
1963	Milwaukee	161	631	121	201	29	4	44	130	.319
1964	Milwaukee	145	570	103	187	30	2	24	95	.328
1965	Milwaukee	150	570	109	181	40	1	32	89	.318
1966	Atlanta	158	603	117	168	23	1	44	127	.279
1967	Atlanta	155	600	113	184	37	3	39	109	.307
1968	Atlanta	160	606	84	174	33	4	29	86	.287
1969	Atlanta	147	547	100	164	30	3	44	97	.300
1970	Atlanta	150	516	103	154	26	1	38	118	.298
1971	Atlanta	139	495	95	162	22	3	47	118	.327
1972	Atlanta	129	449	75	119	10	0	34	77	.265
Major League Totals		2844	10896	1976	3391	572	95	673	2037	.311

Bobby Murcer

Year	Club	G	AB	R	H	2B	3B	HR	RBI	BA
1964	Johnson City	32	126	34	46	7	4	2	29	.365
1965	Greensboro	126	478	95	154	30	5	16	90	.322
	New York	11	37	2	9	0	1	1	4	.243
1966	Toledo	133	492	69	131	19	9	15	62	.266
	New York	21	69	3	12	1	1	0	5	.174
1967	New York			(In Military Service)						
1968	New York			(In Military Service)						
1969	New York	152	564	82	146	24	4	26	82	.259
1970	New York	159	581	95	146	23	3	23	78	.251
1971	New York	146	529	94	175	25	6	25	94	.331
1972	New York	153	585	102	171	30	7	33	96	.292
Major League Totals		642	2365	378	659	103	22	108	359	.279

Johnny Bench

Year	Club	G	AB	R	H	2B	3B	HR	RBI	BA
1965	Tampa	68	214	29	53	13	1	2	35	.248
1966	Peninsula	98	350	59	103	16	0	22	68	.294
	Buffalo	1	0	0	0	0	0	0	0	.000
1967	Buffalo	98	344	39	89	17	2	23	68	.259
	Cincinnati	26	86	7	14	3	1	1	6	.163
1968	Cincinnati	154	564	67	155	40	2	15	82	.275
1969	Cincinnati	148	532	83	156	23	1	26	90	.293
1970	Cincinnati	158	605	97	177	35	4	45	148	.293
1971	Cincinnati	149	562	80	134	19	2	27	61	.238
1972	Cincinnati	147	538	87	145	22	2	40	125	.270
Major League Totals		782	2887	421	781	142	12	154	512	.270

Reggie Jackson

Year	Club	G	AB	R	H	2B	3B	HR	RBI	BA
1966	Lewiston	12	48	14	14	3	2	2	11	.292
	Modesto	56	221	50	66	6	0	21	60	.299
1967	Birmingham	114	413	84	121	26	17	17	58	.293
	Kansas City	35	118	13	21	4	4	1	6	.178
1968	Oakland	154	553	82	138	13	6	29	74	.250
1969	Oakland	152	549	123	151	36	3	47	118	.275
1970	Oakland	149	426	57	101	21	2	23	66	.237
1971	Oakland	150	567	87	157	29	3	32	80	.277
1972	Oakland	135	499	72	132	25	2	25	75	.265
Major League Totals		775	2712	434	700	128	20	157	419	.258

ABOUT THE AUTHOR

Bill Gutman was born in New York City and grew up in Stamford, Connecticut. He was graduated from Washington College with a B.A. in English Literature, and has done graduate work at the University of Bridgeport.

He began his writing career as a reporter and feature writer for *Greenwich Time,* in Greenwich, Connecticut. Soon after, he became the paper's Sports Editor.

He is now a full-time freelance writer specializing in sports. He has written both fiction and non-fiction, working in the book and magazine fields. Among his other books are PISTOL PETE MARAVICH and GREAT QUARTERBACKS, published by Grosset & Dunlap.

He and his wife, Elizabeth, live in Ridgefield, Connecticut.